IT ALL STARTED WITH GOGOL:

Scenes From Life In Russia

IT ALL STARTED WITH GOGOL:

Scenes From Life In Russia

Unusual Experiences In The Soviet Union

THOMAS L. AMAN

Order this book online at www.trafford.com
or email orders@trafford.com

Most Trafford titles are also available at major online book retailers.

Printed in the United States of America.

ISBN: 978-1-4669-4331-5 (sc)
ISBN: 978-1-4669-4330-8 (hc)
ISBN: 978-1-4669-4329-2 (e)

Library of Congress Control Number: 2012911028

Trafford rev. 07/13/2012

 www.trafford.com

North America & international
toll-free: 1 888 232 4444 (USA & Canada)
phone: 250 383 6864 ♦ fax: 812 355 4082

To Tanya, who is so much a part of this book
and my life.

PREAMBLE: WHY RUSSIA?

I am not writing this book about myself, for I simply do not consider that a topic sufficiently interesting to dedicate a book to. However, I have been blessed with an extraordinarily adventurous and interesting life. This book, therefore, is a retelling of some of the experiences I have had, and some of the things that have happened to and around me. I consider myself extremely fortunate to have had these experiences and wish simply to share some of them with anyone who has the interest and the patience to peruse this document further.

It all started with Gogol'. For anyone not familiar with the name, Gogol' was a unique and very talented Russian writer (actually born in Ukraine) who flourished in the early nineteenth century at the beginning of that great moment in Russian history when the country's writers of prose, poetry, and dramaturgy set a mark for creativity that was unprecedented then and never equaled since. I still remember the book well even though I read it well over fifty years ago; the title was *Dead Souls*. It was the drollest, most charming, and unexpectedly unique story I have ever had the pleasure to experience.

Since I didn't know a word of Russian, I read the book in English translation. It hooked me once and for all. With alternating feelings of wonder and awe, I then proceeded to devour in short order most of the works of Dostoevsky, Turgenev, Tolstoy, and Chekhov. For me, it was an epiphany. It immediately became clear to me that if these works were so marvelous in translation, they must be even more stunning and appealing in the language in which they were originally written. I decided to learn Russian. Thus were sown the seeds that would change my life completely and forever.

I spent a number of years studying the language, history, and culture of Russia and the Soviet Union. In 1963, I was given the rare opportunity to study in Moscow as an international exchange scholar. It was certainly an interesting (and not always pleasant) time to be there, but that isn't the subject of this particular commentary. I did manage to learn the language quite well and spent the next several years ingesting virtually all the noteworthy writers of Russia and the Soviet era. My time spent studying the great creative works of the nineteenth and twentieth centuries was equaled only by my attention to the history and culture of this captivating and fascinating land and people. Completing my PhD, I moved to Texas, where I began my internship as a professor of Russian and Soviet studies.

I enjoyed teaching, but somehow it wasn't as fulfilling a vocation as I apparently needed and had imagined. In 1973, I went to New York in search of another opportunity. I found it in the form of a practically unknown, private company that specialized in doing business in the Soviet Union. It was one of only three or so US companies engaged in commerce in that part of the world at that time, therefore, a real rarity. I embraced the company's offer to join their operation with intense enthusiasm and determination. For the next several months, I totally immersed myself in their activities and tried to integrate myself into their Soviet business. About six months after I joined the firm, I began to travel to Moscow on company matters. From that point on, I would travel to the Soviet Union every month or two, in effect spending around half my time there, half my time in the States. My story begins with my travels to Moscow.

One other note: many times in the pages that follow I refer to experiences that occurred "in those days" or "back then." In most cases, I am referring to the period of time roughly from the death of Khrushchev until Yeltsin's reign when the Soviet Union was a very strictly controlled society, almost stultifying in the limitations it attempted to impose on its citizens, and even more so on the foreigners who infrequently visited. However, there was another—much less controlled and far less known—subculture in Moscow that was usually totally closed and unknown to all foreigners, but that will frequently be described in the anecdotes that follow.

INTRODUCTION

Most of the incidents described in the subsequent pages occurred during a time when we—Americans and Soviet citizens—lived with barely suppressed hostility toward one another. Following the Second World War, we ceased being the short-term allies we had become out of necessity and over time became worldwide adversaries. There was a constant if somewhat subtle propaganda waged against the Soviet Union at home while back in Moscow, there was a relentless and unremitting anti-American rhetoric spewed forth to all other districts of the country. With this level of antagonism between us, there was only a diminished level of interest in visiting one another. Nor was it made easy by the authorities to make such a visit—Soviet citizens were simply not allowed to come to the United States (in fact, were not allowed free movement to any other destination), and American visitors had a number of obstacles to calling on their country. Such travelers—be they tourists or businessmen—were uniformly required to have an official invitation from a recognized and officially accepted Soviet organization. All the cities they wished to visit had to be listed and approved, prior hotel arrangements had to be confirmed, and visas had to be obtained. After all these bureaucratic preparations were completed, one had to make travel plans. It was only at that point that the would-be visitor to the Soviet Union would be ready to make his foray into unknown territory.

A major reason I decided to write this compendium of memories is that there exists—or at least used to exist—a deep-seated curiosity about what Russia was really like. This despite the outward hostility that our respective citizens were expected to display, and frequently did display, to each other. The country had been so closed off for so many years that most people had little or no understanding or knowledge of it. Since it was such a dominant force during a majority of those years, scores of people wished to know more about the country that competed with us for world supremacy. The fact that so many citizens were afraid for their very existence because of the mighty threats of the super power and the not so infrequent national crises between us played no small role.

In the following pages, I strive to describe some of the circumstances that occurred and events that I witnessed during countless years of the Cold War. What I felt justified writing them down is that they are so totally different from what most visitors have experienced during their visits to the Soviet Union. The few tourists who ventured into the territory stayed in the best hotels Moscow had to offer; were guided to places like the Tretiakov Gallery, the Bolshoi Theater, and the Kremlin; made fascinating trips to Zagorsk, Borodino, and Izmailovo; and were quite familiar with St. Bazil's Cathedral, the Arbat district, and the famous GUM complex of stores. But I wager that none of them ever experienced the kind of evening I spent once with a local policeman outside the lowly Ostankino Hotel or made the kind of internal trips I made to out-of-the-way places like Zhlobin and Buzuluk or experienced the sort of helicopter sight-seeing tour I was treated to in Almaty. It is because of these fascinating experiences and numerous others I had over the course of many years that I felt it worthwhile to record some of them for curious readers to examine.

THE SOVIET STATE

The Soviet Union was under the complete domination and jurisdiction of a handful of people (overwhelmingly of the male persuasion) who made every decision on how the country was to be run, how society was to be structured, how enterprises and corporations were to be managed, and how everyday people were to live their lives. It was probably the most tightly controlled society in the world, perhaps in the history of nations. The miniscule number of managers and executives made every resolution and ensured—through a massive army and, even more, a huge network of secret agents—that every pronouncement made by government representatives was considered sacrosanct. Moscow executives determined what reading, music, and drama were allowable, and behavior itself was conditioned from early years in school. Soviet government experts considered that the west in general and the United States in particular had one goal in life—the complete overthrow of the Soviet system. They considered us enemies and fought a never-ending war of propaganda to shape and mold the minds of all Soviet citizens. Their chief aim was to have a society comprised of individuals who were totally compliant and acquiescent to the dictates of the state, and the state tried to form its individual citizens into a mass of pliable and submissive inhabitants. Its philosophy was that the more its people feared and hated an outside entity, the less likely it was to demonstrate any resistance to domestic rules and regulations and to show any kind of initiative of its own. The Soviet government made sure that a great deal of the ill will showed by their citizens toward America was in response to this channeling of negative energy in the direction of the west.

There was also not a little envy involved, for those who had some limited access to information from the west knew that people lived a much freer existence with the ability to pursue their own ideas of reading, music, career, ability to move at will, travel, and interact with people of other cultures. These were all missing from the typical Soviet citizen's life options. The dichotomy between what people wanted, therefore, and what was available to them was dramatic, and it was the challenge of the Soviet higher-ups to ensure that the normally placid citizenry not aspire to aspects of life not readily accessible within their system. We were all well aware of this situation, of course, but in a theoretical sense. Seeing it and experiencing it was another matter entirely, but this is what we did from the time of our very first visit to Moscow.

THE FTOS

The company I joined had been doing business with a number of foreign trade organizations which was what the many subsections of the Ministry of Foreign Trade were called. These FTOs (as we referred to them in shorthand) were assigned to initiate and to maintain commercial relations with all foreign companies. They constituted a monopoly in the strictest sense of the word—any foreign company wanting to do business in the Soviet Union had no recourse but to work with one or another of these FTOs. The FTOs controlled absolutely every contact with representatives of foreign companies from initial presentations to technical discussions through all negotiations up to contract signings. They were structured around specific industries so that one would be dedicated to, say, textile machinery, another to automotive, a third to electronic equipment, and so forth. I had been working with a number of American companies which produced agricultural equipment, persuading them that there might be an interesting new market for them in the Soviet Union. The particular FTO responsible for purchasing this type of equipment from abroad (and also selling its own, rather inferior home-grown machinery) was called Tractoroexport. A few of my colleagues had had several meetings with delegates of the FTO and naturally reported back to the rest of us on whom they had met, what had been discussed, and what conclusions drawn. We could then build a consensus on the follow-up required.

Sometime before my second or third trip to Moscow, other colleagues in the company who had had meetings with representatives from Tractoroexport mentioned a certain "Golden Girl." There were two reasons she was given such a moniker—her surname was Zolotova (from the Russian word for gold, *zoloto*), and she had very fine golden blonde hair. I duly took note, for it would be important to follow up a couple projects with her during my next visit to the FTO, and it appeared from the conversation that she was supervising the particular projects our proposals were addressed to resolve.

Working with Soviet organizations in those days was not exactly a joyful experience. You—the foreigner—had to set up all meetings well in advance. No one ever met on the spur of the moment; all meetings were official and all were agreed to ahead of time. The further west you came from, the more official such get-togethers became (or "negotiations" as the Russians called all meetings with foreigners). Typically, the first couple of days in Moscow would involve a few meetings fortuitously arranged before even leaving the United States and the rest of the time plying the phones. The phone system was the worst, most inefficient I had ever experienced. First, there was only one number given out to foreigners for each FTO. FTO departments frequently numbered their employees in the twenties or more, and this meant that nine out of ten attempts at dialing would result in busy signals. In fact, you would often successfully dial only four or five of the seven digits before getting a busy signal. When you finally did make a connection, there was a stronger than fifty-fifty chance that the person you needed was not available. Since whoever picked up the receiver at the FTO knew the caller had to be a foreigner and since all foreigners were by definition antagonists, she/he sometimes simply stated, "Not in." and hung up. Other times you would be told that the individual was in "negotiations." That was actually one of the positive responses: since almost all meetings were limited to an hour or less, it meant that you could try again in an hour and have some chance of getting through. If the answer was "Not at his desk," it meant that the person you needed was in the rest room or in the hall having a cigarette. So you resumed trying after ten minutes or so. The worst response was "Out sick" or "On a business trip" or "On vacation" for you would almost never be told when the individual was expected to reappear. If the person you needed was not there you could ask to leave a message, but you would almost never know if the message was in fact relayed or received. The number of times that someone actually returned my phone call made up a miniscule percentage of total calls. In point of fact, whenever I was in our company suite cum office I was always on the phone myself trying to reach someone in an FTO so that anyone trying to reach me would have had as much difficulty as I had in getting through.

When at last you succeeded in reaching your quarry and requested a meeting, you would frequently be asked, "What is this about?" or "What do you want to discuss?" Assuming that the matter you wished to raise coincided with the interests of the FTO representative you would be assigned a one-hour visitation time—which you didn't dare miss since you probably would not be allotted another in the very near future. When you were able to arrange a meeting, you went to the appointed place—always a little early, for to be late was to forfeit the meeting. Soviet trade officials were very punctual and not terribly patient; they might wait five minutes but never more. The meeting places were always Ministry of Foreign Trade buildings, except in those rare instances when the purpose of the meeting was solely to discuss technical details. In those cases, technical experts from both the Soviet and the foreign side would frequently meet in the relevant industrial ministry. This would give the parties greater flexibility since meeting at a factory would give everyone the opportunity to inspect equipment, for example, determine what problems needed to be resolved and what sort of replacement equipment should be ordered. More importantly, it would take away the one-hour restriction placed on most meeting rooms at the Ministry of Foreign Trade.

But most meetings were at the ministry. You would get there at the agreed upon time, present your credentials to the pair of guards invariably standing at either side of the only entrance, state the name of the person and organization you had come to see, then move aside to allow others entry. Then there was no more to be done other than wait for someone to come fetch you, which happened upon some signal given by one of the guards to the department. Sometimes that someone would be an individual you were actually supposed to meet. However, it was usually a secretary or some other gofer in the department. The secretaries who had clearance to guide foreigners to their meetings were dubbed "correspondents."

When you got to your destination, you were ushered into a small and rather bleak room, typically furnished with a wooden table and two or three straight-backed wooden chairs on each side. You would be invited to take one of the chairs on a specific side of the table. There would always be a used ashtray on the table. Smoking was rampant during these meetings. This accounted for the room almost always being very cold when you got there since someone would mercifully air out the room between meetings. My usual actions while I was waiting for the appointed interlocutors were to take out a full or almost full pack of cigarettes, shake out two or three to make them easy of access and place them near the ashtray, somewhere in the middle of the table. All foreigners learned fairly quickly that locally available cigarettes were looked down upon and that foreign tobacco—especially western in origin—was a treat for all smokers (which seemed to make up 95 percent of the FTO staff if not more).

After a time—usually only a few moments—two people would enter the room. Occasionally, there were variations, such as three individuals joining you, but almost always it was two. They would seat themselves on the other side of the table, and you would know that whoever sat directly opposite you was the senior member of the team. He (rarely she, for the ministry was very male dominated) would be the official spokesman. They would usually introduce themselves almost invariably by surname only and title. If it was not a particularly important gathering, they would be "engineers." A further step up would involve "senior engineers." A more important meeting would bring a deputy director to the table, and a very special negotiation would even witness a director—the most august personality within that department. This would not happen unless the visiting foreigner was a very important person in his own right or if negotiations involved a substantial amount of money and were in the final, crucial phase.

Ministry representatives all graduated from the same school; therefore, they conducted themselves in a more or less similar fashion. They never, or certainly very seldom, smiled and everything they said was completely to the point. There was virtually no small talk, no social chitchat, and no light humor. Their faces were usually very severe, no hint at any softness or individuality as if what was about to transpire was of the utmost solemnity and gravity. Occasionally, a self-important person would enter the room, sit down, and declare, "I'm listening," as if to say, "What do you have to say for yourself? Please don't waste my time." In times like this, you would make a brief presentation, ask a few pertinent questions and try to determine whether there would be any point in asking for a future, follow-up meeting. During all the time, I spent at each meeting I would frequently light up a cigarette, every time inviting my hosts to do likewise. They very rarely refused. I would always "forget" whatever was left in the pack when leaving the room at the end of the meeting. I do not remember a single instance when an FTO representative reminded me to take my "forgotten" cigarettes with me. American cigarettes were a real treat for most Soviets, and I could well imagine my interlocutors dividing up my cigarettes afterward, with the more senior member of the negotiating team getting the lion's share of the booty.

MRS. ZOLOTOVA

I have spent a little time describing what it was like working with Soviet FTOs and their representatives in order to contrast the ordinary, standard way of carrying on business with the way the "Golden Girl" approached matters. When I was next in Moscow, I did call and request a meeting with Mrs. Zolotova. I went through the above-described procedure of arranging a date and time for a get-together. I went to the appointed place a few minutes early, and I was met on the first floor, as was the custom, and conducted upstairs where I was invited to enter the designated room. I took my seat and waited for whoever would show up from the FTO. As soon as Mrs. Zolotova entered the room, I knew that I was due for an unexpected experience. Instead of making the dignified and somewhat dramatic entry customary with most FTO employees, she whisked into the room with the same "correspondent" who had met me downstairs. This almost never happened. Most meetings were hosted by two "engineers"; sometimes one of these would be a "senior engineer" and more rarely a deputy director. As stated earlier, you almost never got to see the venerable director of the department. On the other hand, however, lowly "correspondents" practically never attended negotiations—usually only if everyone else was busy, sick, or on a business trip. Yet all meetings had to have at least two people present, presumably to avoid any possibility of bribery or other attempt to influence commercial decisions. I believe, also, that this was the only time I had ever had a meeting with two women present and no men. Two unusual occurrences at once: two women conducting the meeting and one a "correspondent."

First Meeting

I learned only later that Mrs. Zolotova had somehow connived to have a "correspondent" accompany her so there would not be a more senior witness to the way she conducted her business. She was dressed unlike I had ever seen a representative of a FTO. She had scuffed up loafers on bare feet, a loose fitting blouse of 1940s vintage and baggy pants with a broken drawstring. This caused her to be constantly hiking up her trousers whenever she was not actually sitting. When she entered the room, she proffered her right hand for a handshake. Since this was the one she had been using to keep her pants up, she immediately had to grab her waistband with her left. Even so, her pants fell an inch or two before she rectified the situation. She blushed furiously and since she was extremely fair, this produced a fiery red color on her cheeks. So red and flushed, with one hand determinedly gripping her waistband she briskly advanced toward me and said, "Tatyana," thus stating her given name instead of the standard surname plus title that I was accustomed to hearing. I confess to being somewhat startled at this most unusual turn of events. I introduced myself as I had been advised was proper for foreigners: surname and name of my company. Out of habit, I referred to her as Mrs. Zolotova throughout the meeting despite her having stated only her given name.

I was invited to resume my seat, which I did, the two women taking places directly opposite me. I then immediately offered cigarettes to them—which they showed no hesitation whatsoever in accepting—and lit one up myself. For the next twenty minutes, the two ladies giggled nonstop while the "Golden Girl" joked and filled the atmosphere with humorous small talk. She joked about the weather, the traffic, and the crowds of people—even her trousers. In a word, she was *irreverent*. All other officials I had ever met took every aspect of life in the Soviet Union very seriously. Mrs. Zolotova (Mrs. Z. from now on) apparently found humor in just about everything and refused to accept life as a tragic series of events.

She turned out to be a very bright and attractive woman who seemed completely on top of the several projects we were proposing at that time. We did not accomplish very much at this first meeting. I answered a few questions, brought her up-to-date on the commercial aspects of one major proposal and left technical literature and brochures describing some other equipment. Mrs. Z. suggested that I call in a couple days to see if there were any developments. She indicated that we were reasonably competitive on one of our bids. This was truly unexpected, for normally FTO representatives never gave any hint about the status of your proposal.

Lunch

A few days later my boss, Saul, arrived in Moscow to negotiate with one of our most important and long-standing customers. Before he left the States, he requested that I arrange meetings with these people as well as Mrs. Z. I managed to confirm an appointment with the latter at 10:00 a.m. and the former at 2:00 p.m. on the day after his arrival. We went to the meeting, and Saul met Mrs. Z. for the first time. When our time was up, I was startled to hear Saul invite Mrs. Z. and her colleague, Sasha (a fellow engineer this time, not a "correspondent"), to lunch. She immediately agreed before her companion had a chance to politely refuse. Even more unusual, Saul insisted that they join us for lunch that very day, in fact, in an hour's time. Soviet officials were not frequently invited out for they were simply not allowed to socialize freely with foreigners. Thus, about the only occasions when they were allowed to accept an invitation was, for example, when a contract was to be celebrated. Even these events were tightly monitored and permission was always required before hand. Also, I had never known Saul to invite anyone on such short notice or when there was no particular business event to commemorate. It showed an impulsive side to his character that I hadn't been aware of previously. It also showed that when Mrs. Z. wanted something she had no hesitation about breaking a few rules to get it.

Came 12:00 noon and we descended to the ground floor of the hotel where the restaurant was located. Sure enough, Mrs. Z. and

Sasha were there waiting for their hosts. We all took seats at the table showed to us, Saul and I on one side, our guests on the other. It was the most unusual business lunch I had attended up to that point. In fact, there was virtually no talk of business. Saul was a very bright man and very patient. Mrs. Z.'s English was not too refined and Sasha's not much better. But rather than have me translate Saul would speak very slowly, enunciating each word very carefully, sometimes choosing another, simpler, word to convey his thoughts. On the other hand, when Mrs. Z. spoke, he patiently helped her find the words she was looking for. Sasha and I took very little part in the conversation. Mrs. Z. had a way of expressing herself that could best be described as quirky. She would use the most unusual words at times, their juxtaposition resulting in some very humorous moments. Yet they weren't artful in the sense that she was deliberately trying to be funny; they were, in fact, quite spontaneous, and it wasn't just struggling in a foreign language. Later, when she began speaking Russian to me, and even later, when she became very accomplished in English, I learned that she spoke that way all the time regardless of the language she used. For example, where most people would say "Too bad," or "That's awful!" she might murmur, "How mournful." Or when asked how her day had gone, where most would say, "Great," or "Wonderful!" she might state, "Simply beatific." She was full of delight and joy, had humorous opinions about everything, and refused to take any Soviet strictures seriously. I could tell that Saul was simply captivated. I should point out here that Saul was in his early seventies, and Mrs. Z was in her late twenties.

The lunch went well, but after an hour and a half it came time for Saul and me to leave for our two o'clock meeting. I nudged him and whispered that we had to excuse ourselves and depart immediately so as not to be late. Saul whispered back that I should attend alone and report back to him when I returned to the hotel. I responded that after the two o'clock event I had several other commitments that would keep me tied up until around 6:00 p.m. He advised that that would be just fine; he would see me upon my return. I was absolutely astounded: the meeting at 2:00 p.m. was the main reason he had come to Moscow in the first place, and never before had I known him to miss a meeting with these particular clients. I did the best I could on my own, attended the other negotiations I had committed to and returned to the hotel about 6:30 p.m. A few minutes to clean up and I went to the suite we used as an office. No answer, so this meant Saul had gone downstairs for an early dinner. I went down to join him and report on my activities.

If I was astounded when he declined to attend the two o'clock meeting, the sight that greeted me as I entered the restaurant totally flabbergasted me. There was Saul and across the table from him were still sitting Mrs. Z. and Sasha. He invited me to join them, and there the four of us spent the rest of the evening. As incredible as the entire situation seemed to me at the time, it was, nevertheless, a most enjoyable evening. We had a nice meal with a little wine, and I sat back and contented myself with observing Mrs. Z. and Saul. They were having a wonderful time, bantering and joking as if they had been friends for years, and the venue were London instead of Moscow. Sasha took about as much part in the conversation as I did, that is to say, almost none. But it was fun to watch and listen. A few hours later, everyone agreed that we had probably better part company for the evening. Before saying final farewells, however, Saul invited the two of them to the restaurant of their choice for Saturday evening. Mrs. Z. agreed with considerable alacrity, so we were on for the date in a couple days' time. In response to Saul's question of where they would like to go she indicated that she would like to go to a restaurant called the Rus'.

The Rus'

A major challenge in Moscow back then was to find something interesting to do during leisure time. Since my boss normally kept me busy twelve to fifteen hours a day during the workweek, leisure time was, by definition, weekends or local holidays. We usually tried to avoid making trips to Moscow during the latter since with the Russians' penchant for celebrating, it was not only the holiday itself, but also frequently a period of some days both before and after the official holiday that was lost to us while our would-be Russian hosts made merry. And since we usually tried to make weekends our travel days, we only had to suffer the weekends in Moscow when on extended trips. Thus, whenever a new form of entertainment or stylish dining establishment opened, we would try to work it in. A short time before I met Mrs. Z., I heard rumor of an interesting new restaurant/bar that had opened just outside the city proper. The name of the new place was Rus' (the ancient and historical name for Russia itself), and it was reputed to be the most "in" place within an acceptable traveling distance from central Moscow. I didn't know Mrs. Z. very well at this point, but I had already become sufficiently accustomed to her zest and enthusiasm that her choice of this new establishment did not surprise me.

To get to the restaurant, you had to drive some distance out of the city itself along the not inappropriately named "Highway of Enthusiasts." The restaurant complex was located a small distance off the main highway. As you approached, there was forest on all sides, quiet and serene, free from the noise and toxicity of Moscow's traffic and industrial plants. Two main buildings were situated among bountiful and luxuriant snow-covered trees a short distance from the highway. One was the restaurant proper, a fairly large structure accommodating probably a hundred or more customers. The other was a combination bar and private rooms catering to the upper echelons of the hierarchy. Arriving visitors would approach from the left of the restaurant, enter a small vestibule, and after getting past the ubiquitous maître d', be ushered into a vast hall with numerous tables and a bandstand overlooking a dance floor. Mrs. Z. had whispered to me that I should have a twenty-ruble note ready for, despite the fact that we had reservations, such information could be lost unless one provided incentive. The twenty got us a bright smile from the maître d' and an immediate invitation into the hall proper to a beautifully set table for four. Obviously an appropriate incentive.

In a repeat of a couple days ago, we took our seats with Mrs. Z. and Sasha assuming places on one side of the table, Saul and I on the other. Again, Saul and Mrs. Z. began to engage in small talk. This time, however, it was different from our earlier lunch. Sasha continued to play a very passive role, seemingly content to spend his time observing the rest of us, and I deferred to Saul's apparent desire to converse with the young woman. But Mrs. Z. began to pull me more and more into her dialogue with him. It was a delightful evening, very light and humorous, full of happy stories, jokes, and anecdotes. We ate, drank, and began to tell a little about our families and ourselves and what paths we had taken to arrive at that particular place in time. In short, it was an entirely unique experience. The simple fact was that Soviet citizens were very much discouraged from cultivating social or personal relationships, and indeed, could suffer severe consequences (both professional and personal) from such relationships with foreigners.

When Soviets went out to dinner, it was an event that required an entire evening. Reservations were an absolute requirement because of the enormous demand and the relatively small number of first-rate restaurants. To show up at a restaurant without reservations meant one of two things—either a placard would be hanging on the entrance proclaiming that the place was closed or a maître d' would open the door a crack just wide enough for the prospective guest to pass through a hefty enticement. Since dinner was an all-evening affair, restaurant guests entertained themselves with copious eating and drinking interspersed by dancing. Dancing in Moscow was always interesting to observe: it was enthusiastic to say the least and primordial when the evening wore on and people got more and more animated with drink and happy conversation. The frequently boisterous music created an outlet for Russians' natural exuberance plus freely flowing alcohol tended to lessen their inhibitions.

Not too long after we took our seats, the band appeared and immediately launched into some very modern western rock and roll. I was dumbfounded. In the time, I had been coming to Moscow, I had never heard anything like this—it was positively blasphemous. All good restaurants played music, but all those in which I had dined played only standard, stodgy Soviet style music or safe western tunes from the 1940s and 1950s. To hear roaring and raucous rock music blaring out of the loudspeakers of a Soviet-era restaurant was so unique as to be startling. At the time, such music was considered downright decadent by officious authorities and was virtually unheard-of. Indeed, there were probably not a few Soviet officials who, in their zeal, would have pushed to have the Rus' managers prosecuted had they known of the irreverence proliferating just outside the Moscow city limits.

Tanya

After a time, I was surprised to see Mrs. Z. get up from her seat and approach me. She mockingly asked if all young American men ignored their women guests and indicated that she expected me to invite her to dance. When we got to the dance floor she made two things immediately clear to me: she openly chided me for not being more sociable to her, that is, had not asked her to dance with me, and insisted that from now on I should call her Tanya. Though I am not a particularly accomplished dancer,

Tanya (for that is how I called her from this moment on except in very official circumstances) made things easy for me. She kept moving but distracted me from my clumsy efforts with a constant chatter that was animated, witty, and vivacious—the opposite of official conversation in Moscow back then. But I had to admit this get-together was anything but official from the very beginning. Her cheeks were flushed, her soft golden hair bounced as we whirled around, her eyes were lit up like sparklers, and her smile was perpetual. I may not have been as thoroughly enchanted as Saul was, but I confess to finding this young woman extremely attractive and interesting and enjoyed every moment with her.

We finished a couple numbers and returned to the table. Just in good time, I believe, because Saul and Sasha were by now struggling to communicate with each other and a rather heavy silence had descended over the twosome. On the way back to join the others, Tanya hinted pointedly that I should not make her take the initiative in asking her to dance later. But no more than five minutes passed, before Saul gallantly invited her to dance. Now it was Sasha's and my turn to try to socialize a bit. This did not go too well since he was rather stiff and somewhat officious. However, I gave it a great effort and somehow we managed to converse a little until the others returned, and so it went the remainder of the evening. Now Saul and Tanya heading off to the dance floor, now she and I taking a turn to the decidedly un-Soviet type music. Never did Sasha show the slightest inclination to participate. He was simply there, an observer. Only once did he rise and invite Tanya to join him—but not to the dance floor, just to a far corner of the room where they briefly spoke to one another in a low tone of voice. Later, I discovered that he was cautioning Tanya on her behavior—she should not be so open and sociable with foreigners. Still later I learned that Sasha was only one of the numerous KGB agents assigned to the FTO.

Rizo

At one point during this extraordinary evening I waited to the end of a set and approached the bandleader to congratulate him on how well he and his colleagues played. He was effusive in his thanks and, without hesitation, invited me to join him where he rested between sets together with his colleagues. It turned out that this place was a very small room situated directly beneath the stage itself and accessible through a tiny opening that I did not even realize existed until we went through it. Its ceiling was the underside of the stage and so low that we had to bend over to enter the room and stay that way during the remainder of our time there. My host introduced himself as Rizo and I gave him my name. He was a small Armenian, probably no more than 5'4" very wiry, swarthy in appearance, with a great hooked nose and tight, curly black hair. He had the blackest eyes I ever saw, but they held a glimmer of humor and warmth that immediately created a very easy atmosphere between us. The lead singer and guitarist was a Russian by the name of Zhenya. They showed me to a little rickety straight-backed chair and seated themselves in two identical ones. We sat around an equally flimsy miniature table. Very shortly, a mostly full bottle of brandy materialized from somewhere, and we soon were toasting our acquaintance. I spent a very pleasurable fifteen minutes or so with the musicians before they had to excuse themselves to perform for the restaurant guests.

During the course of the evening, they invited me to join them three or four more times, and over the next few years, I was to visit them on a fairly frequent if irregular basis and probably made dozens of trips to their little lair beneath the stage. We invariably sipped brandy, told each other about music trends in our respective countries, talked a little about ourselves, our work, our hobbies, friends, families, and so forth. As far as I knew then I might have been the only foreigner ever invited there; at least I never saw anyone else duck down into the little opening or emerge from there. I took to sometimes giving them little presents as a miniscule reward for their hospitality, and especially, for the wonderful music they played and I enjoyed. Once I presented them with a special recording of the Credence Clearwater Revival (CCR) group. The next time I came to the club they did several of the CCR songs—perfectly. It was the most faultless rendition of CCR that I could imagine—other than the famed musicians themselves. I was always astounded at their ability to vocalize English lyrics with perfect pronunciation, intonation, and diction—when not a single band member knew more than two words of the language. Their greatest lament was the creative restrictions placed on all musicians in the Soviet Union by bureaucrats who knew everything about filling out forms and signing papers but nothing about melodies and lyrics, tempo and beat.

Tanya's History

We spent the remainder of the evening in this most pleasant environment. When the time grew late enough so that we all realized we should call it a night, we departed, intending first to drop Tanya off, then Sasha, then to deliver Mr. Rosenbaum, and myself back to our hotel. Upon our arrival to Tanya's apartment building, she invited me to walk her to her flat, but Sasha insisted on accompanying her. Though she resisted this to some extent Sasha prevailed. Later, I learned that as the KGB representative among us he felt the need to remonstrate her for her behavior and to seek assurances that it would not be repeated. Such fraternizing with Westerners as Tanya could have been accused of was simply not considered professional behavior in official circles; some might even have deemed it as bordering on traitorous. However, the future would show that Sasha had no idea whom he was reckoning with. In this relatively quiet way concluded my most memorable evening in Moscow to date. Shortly thereafter, Tanya began to find increasingly creative ways for us to see each other, first with Rosenbaum as "business" colleague, then just the two of us, and so began a relationship that grew closer and closer as the months and years went by.

Viktor

Tanya had been married about eight years when we first met. Over a substantial period of time, I learned a great deal about her relationship with her husband, Viktor. They had been classmates for many years in the physics department of a very demanding and very prestigious university, the alma mater of many of the Soviet Union's foremost nuclear physicists. The university was a natural springboard for anyone intelligent enough to handle the rigors of extremely tough scholastic standards and ambitious enough to aim for an exacting scientific and technical career. However, it took serious clout to get accepted into a program at the university, very conscientious and dedicated work to complete the highly demanding course work, and an advanced level of native intelligence. Both Tanya and Viktor possessed the first ingredient of this formula and that is how they found themselves classmates.

The second and third ingredients were a little more complicated. Viktor definitely did not have the natural tools to negotiate all the course work successfully. Left to his own devices, he would have been forced to leave the school without graduating. Tanya, on the other hand, had sufficient intelligence and a high enough level of ambition to see her through without a problem. By dint of diligent effort and a great deal of pushing (not to mention help on exams) she also managed to get Viktor graduated as well. They decided to marry during this romantic phase. They were young, definitely somewhat immature, and held the mistaken but typical belief that their feelings for each other were deep, genuine and strong enough to last permanently.

Viktor was tall and thin, handsome with dark hair and possessed a Hollywood-like face and an easygoing grace. He was a very talented individual—quite accomplished at drawing and painting, he could play the guitar and sing a myriad of songs, spoke several languages well, and could tell jokes and anecdotes with a dry wit and seemingly without end. Though somewhat superficial, he was a hit in just about every social assemblage. Tanya was also very adept at social communion, so it transpired that the two of them became very popular among young groups gathering together for letting off steam from the pressures of seeking success in the difficult Soviet environment.

Their careers took a rather unexpected direction when Tanya insisted on entering the Ministry of Foreign Trade instead of following through on her education in nuclear physics. She was able to secure an interview by dint of her father's connections that were both numerous and powerful, and her natural intelligence and vivacious wit carried her through the interview process in a breeze. Viktor, who had been coached through all the most difficult courses and helped through the exams, never possessed the knowledge or the skills or even the desire to pursue a career in nuclear physics. He ended up with an entry-level position in the secretariat of the Komsomol (the Youth Communist League). It turned out that he had the requisite qualities to become a gifted bureaucrat who laboriously and cautiously worked his way up the ladder over the years to attain a high-ranking job within the organization.

Marriage

Like so many young people without an abundance of worldly experience, Tanya and Viktor decided to marry despite the misgivings of Tanya's father. Their life at home turned sour very soon after the marriage. Tanya became pregnant almost immediately, and with pregnancy was ill and out of sorts a great deal of the time. Viktor was essentially a very shallow and superficial person, whereas Tanya was a very caring and warm individual. Her emotions ran deep, whereas Viktor was always most at home and content when entertaining friends. Tanya was "no fun" anymore. Consequently, he more and more frequently left her to her own devices while he went out to visit with friends. Thus began a pattern for the young married couple: Viktor going to work every day, then oftentimes partying and visiting with friends in the evening. Tanya, on the other hand, stayed home most days and evenings because of her pregnancy-related infirmity, only occasionally punctuating this boring and unpleasant existence with visits to her family. Their relationship grew colder and more distant. They stopped any pretense at intimacy and began to relate to one another with ill-concealed hostility. During pretty much the remainder of Tanya's pregnancy, they kept aloof from one another and barely maintained the pretense of civility.

Anya's Birth

When time drew near for the baby's delivery, Tanya moved in with her parents. A month later, she was admitted to the hospital where she endured a short but very painful and complicated labor and then delivered a little girl. Regarding the naming of the child Viktor had earlier acceded to Tanya's request. If it was a boy, they would name it after her father. If it was a girl, after her grandmothers since both had the same name. And so it transpired that Viktor and Tanya had a baby girl whose name became Anna or, variously, Anya, Anyuta, or Anichka. From the very beginning, Anya was sickly and frail, thus, according to Soviet medical custom, Tanya and the baby were released from the hospital only after a period of nine days. In the interim, both her father and Viktor came to visit every day—even though neither was allowed to have any physical contact with either Tanya or Anya. In one of those intriguing psychological anomalies, Viktor, despite his total indifference toward Tanya, showed an immediate and intense love for Anya.

When mother and baby were allowed to go home, they went to Tanya's parents' apartment to live. Viktor also moved in so as to be closer to the object of his adoration. However, the baby was not well from the very beginning and spent most of her waking hours crying despite everyone's best efforts to comfort her. This set of circumstances lasted for the next year and amounted to pure hell for all five people, for the quarters were small and cramped, and even the tiniest sound could be heard from one end of the apartment to the other. Yet they all felt it was necessary since Tanya could not possibly have coped with Anya alone.

After a year, it was decided that Viktor and Tanya should move back to their apartment and leave Anya with her grandmother. Since Viktor was earning very little at his low-ranking bureaucrat position everyone believed that it would be best if Tanya went back to work to help improve the overall financial situation. Her mother would look after the baby in the meantime until some other solution could be found. Living apart was no option because of the housing scarcity in Moscow. Since they were forced to share their tiny apartment, and since their relationship had deteriorated even further than previously was the case, they divided it by proclaiming the kitchen and bathroom as common territory with the other two rooms designated one for Viktor and one for Tanya.

Marriage Breakup

There were two significant things that occurred over the next interim period—Viktor started getting physically abusive toward Tanya, and she began earning enough money to stay at work full time and hire a nanny to care for Anya. This would allow the baby to be returned to its parents and at the same time free up Tanya's mother so she could resume working. Viktor desperately wanted his daughter to be at home; so Tanya was able to use this fact to leverage Viktor into promising to cease his physical abuse of her if she allowed Anya to live with them. And so they began their strange family relationship—the three of them together for the first time since Anya's birth and without others around. Yet they were not really together since Tanya and Viktor continued to occupy separate rooms. Now, however, both parents worked and both had access to the baby every evening. The financial arrangements were rather lopsided. Viktor contributed only the bare essential monetary support to feed Anya each month. Tanya took care of the rest of the baby's needs, all of her own, the cost of a full-time nanny, as well as all costs associated with renting an apartment in Moscow at that time.

And so this negative existence continued for quite some period of time. Anya's status seemed to improve or, at least, she cried and fussed a lot less, began to eat fractionally better, and a certain calm came into their lives. As the baby turned into a small child, she began to show signs of turning into quite an extraordinary little girl. She began talking at a very early age and quite soon was not just speaking solitary isolated words with poor pronunciation, but complete sentences with perfect enunciation. While she was developing her mind and limbs, the adults worked out a primitive compromise between themselves. They stayed in their separate rooms with Anya sleeping in Tanya's room, and shared the child during their free time. They spoke to one another only when necessary and, otherwise, had absolutely no contact whatsoever.

Viktor became ever more distant from Tanya, but his love and devotion to Anya were boundless. He spent hours with her showing her how to draw and paint, playing the guitar and singing to her. She picked things up amazingly fast, and within a few years she was a superior artist, especially excelling at depictions of animals. She learned lyrics and melody and enjoyed singing to the applause of whatever adults were present for her impromptu performances. She memorized lengthy poems and was always pleased to recite—which she did with perfect diction and never a mistake. Somewhere she developed a deep hunger to learn about mythology, and as soon as she was able to read—which she started doing at a very early age—she devoured everything she could get her hands on about the Greek and Roman gods.

Tanya's time with her daughter was different. They would talk about everything, take long walks in the park, and visit the zoo at every opportunity. They would spend great chunks of time at Tanya's parents with the grandparents—especially her grandfather—regaling her with tales of people he had met, things he had done, and adventures he had experienced, foreign countries he had been posted in. While in the park or zoo or out at the dacha, Tanya noticed that Anya seemed to have acquired a very special characteristic. She had developed an extraordinary affinity for animals. Wild birds would fly right up to her and perch next to her on the bench. Normally vicious dogs would lie down at her feet and whimper for a little affection. At their country home, she would pet the goat that was usually mean and skittish, and he would relish it, whereas he wouldn't let anyone else even near. So Anya's affinity for art and her love for animals came together in the most wonderful pictures of animals she would spend hours dallying over. She most particularly loved horses and could draw and paint them in all imaginable attitudes—standing, lying down, running, and jumping. She could even give them human qualities—one would have a sly smile on its face, another would wink, a third would hold a smoldering cigarette between its lips (all Soviets seemed to smoke—including both Tanya and Viktor). Very creative, very clever, and very well done. She once drew and colored a caricature of me, which showed an alligator in upright position with a briefcase in one hand and a cane in the other, all decked out in suit, vest, and tie. The alligator's face bore an uncanny resemblance to my own.

They carried on in this fashion for some years. Anya turned into a lovely, warm, and affectionate little girl. She was also smart as a whip and, in short order, became the hero of the family. Her talent in so many areas made her a pleasure to be around. Everyone in their apartment complex remarked on her abilities, and when she started school, she soon made many more friends. Tanya and Viktor simply basked in their pride of Anya, and Tanya's parents were practically demented from love for the child. As everyone expected, she excelled at her studies and even her teachers couldn't heap enough praise on her.

As I got to know Tanya better, spent more and more time with her and learned about her family, and as our relationship brought us ever closer to one another, it seemed that meeting her family members and gaining firsthand knowledge of them was inevitable. From long conversations with Tanya, I had learned that, in addition to Anya, her family consisted of grandparents, a much beloved sister, her mother and father.

TANYA'S FAMILY

I have many times reflected on how fortunate I was in having chosen Tanya. Not only did I find the one woman, I would love and cherish the rest of my life, but her family became almost as close to me as my own. You love your own parents, but you don't get to choose them. Here I was in a situation where I got to love my parents-in-law, and they loved me in turn without qualification. I shall never forget Tanya's mother once saying to me, "Tom, I've loved only three men in my life: my father, my husband, and you." And Tanya's sister, Galya? She's been like a younger sister to me since well before Tanya and I got married.

Tanya's mother and grandmother were true Russian hero-women. They recognized nothing other than husband, family, and never-ending toil. This is what made up their world. Like the Russian women of old immortalized in many of the works of famous authors, they were unbelievably tough, determined, and loyal. They had gone through revolution and civil war, a Nazi invasion, famine, a despotic regime, and untold years of unremitting labor. Yet they remained unfazed, unbroken, and unashamed. I always had great respect for Tanya's mother who showed her true worth during the war years digging trenches, carrying arms and ammunition to the soldiers, and tending to the wounded. In short, she did whatever was required in the spirit of sacrifice for which Russian women had for centuries been famous. Grandmother was one of the hardest working people I have ever met. Not only did she help build their modest little home from the ground up, she tended the goats and chickens, took flowers to the roadside market for selling, and grew everything possible on their little plot of land. Tomatoes, radishes, onions, carrots, beets, and scallions were only a small selection of the many vegetables they grew. Then whatever was not consumed at the time of harvest, she preserved for utilization in the winter. Over and above the daily grind was their love for the youngest members of their family. In their case, it was the devotion specifically and intensively lavished on Anya. From the moment she was born Anya was the object of pure adoration for Tanya's mother and other immediate relatives.

Tanya's sister, Galya, was a sweet, bright, and good-natured girl married to a young man named Seriozha. He was a career bureaucrat trapped in the gigantic organization responsible for setting and regulating state standards. Though his job was stultifying, he himself was a witty and humorous chap who found amusement in just about every unofficial situation. He had a real talent for the clever use of words, and I always found great pleasure in conversing with him—as long as the subject was relatively light-hearted. Galya was generous and caring; she was warm and outgoing. She had a special relationship with all the family members and was never contentious or argumentative. She and Seriozha had a child of their own, a son named Andriusha. Though he was younger than Anya, he worshiped her and followed her around like a little puppy always ecstatic over the slightest sign of attention. Anya was the daughter Galya never had, so it was natural that her attachment to the little girl was unrestrained. She and Tanya had a very special relationship that involved devotion, loyalty, and a boundless empathy toward each other. Their love can only be described as limitless and inexhaustible. However, if one can make the distinction, whereas Tanya cared very deeply for her sister, she simply adored her father. Since he was such an important member of the family, he deserves special mention at this stage in my remembrances.

NIKOLAI IVANOVICH

Tanya's father was clearly the dominant figure in the household. He had been inducted into the army as a nineteen-year-old youth in 1941 and fought four arduous years until the German forces were finally beaten back. He had been wounded seriously four times and was one of only half-a-dozen of his fellow inductees in his battalion of cannon fodder riflemen pitted against German tanks to survive the war. A highly decorated officer in the Red Army, he had retired shortly before Tanya and I met. His name was Nikolai Ivanovich (I shall refer to him as NI from here on) and he tended to make a pronounced and immediate impression on one.

My Relationship with Tanya

When he first heard from Tanya that she was seeing a man other than her husband, he was more than just a little disgruntled. When he was further advised that this man was a foreigner, he became very disturbed. When he learned that this foreigner was an American, he was beside himself. He quickly and forcibly forbade Tanya from ever seeing me again. He forgot, however, Tanya's lineage. If NI was forceful, headstrong, and determined, Tanya was every bit his match. By this time, we had already been seeing each other for some time and both of us realized that our association had already become close, was gaining momentum, and that neither of us wanted it to end. There was no way that Tanya was going to forsake our relationship to appease her father—despite her very real respect for his wishes and desire to do his bidding.

Thus began a war of wits and stubbornness between the two. The other family members stayed in the background although they did not disguise their opposition to our continuing association. They unambiguously sided with NI, which made Tanya's situation regarding her family exceedingly fragile and increasingly unpleasant. Her mother was a very demonstrative person, frequently given to extraordinary displays of emotion regardless of the circumstances. On one occasion, she and Tanya were going someplace in Moscow via the subway system—which was always crowded—and discussing our relationship. At one point, Tanya's mother got so agitated that she fell to her knees in front of hundreds of other passengers, let her very abundant hair down to her waist, and launched into an extremely verbal and public curse on her daughter for the evil she was perpetrating in consorting with an American.

NI tended to be much calmer and more composed, but this did not signify that he was any less opposed to our seeing each other or less determined to see an end to it. On the contrary, he began to threaten Tanya with denouncing her to the personnel department (read KGB) at her place of employment. In those days, consorting with a foreigner, especially an American, was practically tantamount to treason and would be punished by immediate dismissal from employment and possibly worse. Not that NI would actually have carried out the threat; he simply wanted to frighten her into forfeiting any future relationship with me. Tanya was adamant, however, and refused to yield to this verbal extortion.

So NI tried another tactic. I was at my desk in our company suite at the Hotel Berlin doing some paperwork one day when there was a telephone call. I lifted the receiver and pronounced my name. The voice at the other end asked, "Do you know who this is?" With a certain dread I recognized that it was Tanya's father despite never having met him or heard his voice. My heart instantly plummeted to the bottom of my stomach, and I broke out in a cold sweat. When I replied in the affirmative, he said very distinctly and clearly, "If you do not stop seeing my daughter I will make all necessary arrangements to prevent you from ever receiving another visa to the Soviet Union. You will never be able to come to Moscow again. Do you understand what I have said?" By now, I was trembling from a combination of fright and outrage—fright over the fact that I knew he could actually accomplish what he threatened, and outrage that he was interfering so directly in Tanya's and my relationship.

After a slight pause, I replied as courteously as I could that "Yes, I understand the words you have spoken, but I most respectfully do not accept what you have said. Your daughter and I care very much for each other, and I truly hope that you will take that into consideration and do nothing as drastic as you have described."

His reply was short and chilling, "You will be sorry for what you are doing." After which he hung up. I was totally unnerved and told Tanya all about the conversation when we next got together. Neither of us could think of any remedy to the situation. She promised to try and mollify her father; I could do no more than hope for the best. Shortly thereafter, I had to return to the States. When we parted, we did not even know whether or not we would ever see each other again.

I returned to the States where the next month to six weeks—my normal cycle of trips between NY and Moscow—were full of trepidation. I filed all the proper applications for visa and hotel voucher without having any idea whether they would be granted. I realized that, despite my having done absolutely nothing illegal, NI could easily have reported me to the KGB. Had he denounced me they could simply have blacklisted me, thus precluding any future visas and effectively blocking any and all visits to the Soviet Union on my part from that point on. Nevertheless, I submitted all the relevant paperwork and hoped for the best. In this particular case, everything seemed to turn out positively; all the official papers required were delivered to me within a normal period of time. This did not, however, eliminate all my concerns. I was very anxious over what might await me after arriving in Moscow.

Request for Meeting

I traveled to Moscow at the appointed time and started my normal practice of telephone calls, meetings, and seeing Tanya whenever possible. Soon, however, there was a decided difference. After I had been in town two or three days, Tanya announced that NI wanted to meet with me personally. This news filled me with considerable dread if not downright dismay. The next few days were consumed with delicate negotiations on where and when we would meet and under what circumstances. I pressed Tanya to predict what NI would try to accomplish at such a meeting and to guess what kinds of things he would ask about and whether he would threaten me again. She was as troubled as I about the future of our relationship, but could offer no more advice than simply to be myself and act as naturally as possible under extremely unsettling circumstances.

The day arrived when we were supposed to have the momentous meeting. Tanya had coached me on the type of spirits I should offer NI, and I had obediently purchased an expensive bottle of cognac. Since NI had expressly stated that the interview would include only the two of us, Tanya had arranged for her sister, Galya, to keep her company. No one had the faintest idea of whether the encounter would last five minutes or five hours. The designated venue for the meeting was Tanya's apartment. I arrived half an hour ahead of time in case Tanya had any final words of advice. At the designated time, a taxi arrived and discharged NI and Galya. Ten minutes later, after introducing NI and me to each other and setting out a few items of food, two glasses, and the bottle of cognac, Tanya seated the two of us at the table in her living room and departed with Galya.

Our First Get Together

NI was an impressive figure. He was not tall, probably no more than five feet eight or nine, but he was very solid; although dressed in a suit he appeared not to have an ounce of fat or flab on his frame. He had very thick shoulders and strong hands and seemed anchored to the floor with two tree-trunk like legs. His waist was ample but not soft. His hair was brown turning to gray and rather sparse so that two very prominent indentations were immediately visible, one on his forehead and another a little further back. These were two of the four prominent scars he carried from wounds suffered in the war. It was obvious that either of the two visible scars represented wounds that might have been fatal if incurred an inch or two in another direction. NI had very bright brown eyes that looked at you steadfastly and unflinchingly. I admit to having felt a bit unnerved at his unblinking stare. He had thick lips and a very proud Roman nose. Overall, NI projected a most imposing presence.

We sat and looked at each other—warily, I suppose, for we probably considered ourselves more antagonists than potential friends. It was fairly quiet at first, then we began to talk. He started asking me questions—what kind of family I was from, what did my father do, in what did my work consist, how did I happen to speak Russian. I told him about my rather modest roots, my life on the farm, my parents, brothers, and sister, three sons, and my abiding and long-standing fondness for and interest in all things Russian. I told him my story of how it all started with Gogol. As the afternoon wore on, we consumed Tanya's snacks, partook liberally of the cognac, and continued talking about everything except politics.

NI turned out to be a fascinating man. In time, he narrated a tale of having served several years in the war, suffered multiple serious wounds, later worked in military intelligence, traveled a fair share of the world and met heads of state, ministers, and other high-ranking individuals in both the Soviet Union and foreign lands. He also proved to be a polite and attentive listener. He seemed genuinely interested to hear about my family, my work, and my fascination with Russian culture and history. He asked many questions, but always courteously and quietly—never aggressively. The climate between us slowly developed from cool to cautious to warm. By the time, Tanya and Galya returned—fully five hours after they had bid us good-bye and good luck—NI and I had settled into an easy and relaxed relationship. The ladies were astounded but extremely happy at the somewhat unexpected turn of events. When I accompanied NI and Galya out to the street to catch a taxi awhile later, he embraced me and told me how pleased he was to make my acquaintance and how much he hoped to see me again soon. Over the following years that Tanya and I continued our courtship, got married, and began getting together socially with her family on every possible occasion, NI and I became close friends. We gradually started to do many different things and go places as a twosome.

He would take me to a variety of fascinating places. We attended important soccer and hockey matches where it was imperative that we always root for the Red Army team—his favorite, of course. We went out for lunch together to a little known establishment where he knew the waiters and the maître d' and we received very special service because of his status as a veteran. He once invited me to the apartment of a friend of his—a former ambassador to a prominent African nation. I shall never forget the residence. It confirmed to me what I had always guessed but had never observed personally: that privileged individuals in the Soviet Union had access to perks that the common people did not. The apartment was spacious and furnished with luxurious accoutrements, including a collection of artifacts from Africa that was probably worth a fortune. We went skating together and took long walks under the gray Moscow skies, copious snowflakes accumulating on our heads and shoulders, faces rosy from the effort and the cold. We talked about everything—our families, life in the Soviet Union and America, his duty during the war, my work, and Tanya's and my relationship. I guess I ended up being the son he always wanted but never had. I was always proud of the fact that this product of Soviet culture could take a total outsider—a foreigner at that—into his heart and grow to love him like his very own son, and indeed, NI did treat me like his son.

THE DACHA AND DED

After Tanya and I were married, I became a firmly established member of the family. As such, it was only a matter of time before I was invited to their dacha. The Russian word *dacha* signifies country home or cottage. However, whereas our notion of cottage frequently conjures up a nifty little place on a lake or near a beach, a typical Russian dacha is most likely many miles away from large bodies of water. We tend to think of cottage as an escape from the city on weekends and possibly a week or two in the summer. It is often a place for swimming, sailing, fishing, and a myriad of other water-related sports. It usually has many amenities such as comfortable sleeping accommodations for several guests, indoor plumbing, electricity, and sometimes central heating for year-round use. Most travel to the cottage is on well-paved roads.

A Russian Dacha

A Russian family's dacha is very often located in close proximity to others in open fields noteworthy for their paucity of trees. Other, more fortuitous owners locate their dacha in the forest—the latter, of course, being far preferable to the former. When truly good luck (or finances) favors a family, their dacha can be located not too distant from a river or a pond. This occasionally gives them the possibility to fish or to swim, although in a somewhat restricted fashion. Dachas frequently have no electricity or heating system other than a wood-burning stove, no indoor plumbing, and are usually very limited in size. It is frequently necessary to negotiate many kilometers of rough, unpaved road to gain access. As often as possible—invariably where space permits—Russians maintain a vegetable garden, which goes a long way toward supplementing their regular food supply. The garden is also frequently a small source of extra income since many dacha owners grow flowers—which they then sell at whatever cemetery or bazaar is located nearby—as well as fruits and vegetables which are flogged alongside any conveniently located roadway. Dachas are meeting places for many family members, relatives, and friends on weekends and holidays when they can retreat from the anxiety and stress of the urban workplace. They are frequently the center for "letting down one's hair" as in abundant intake of food and beverages.

Although the dacha is usually considered fundamentally a sanctuary from the heat and toxicity of the city in the summertime, not all Russians have the luxury of utilizing it only as an escape. In fact, across the country literally hundreds of thousands of citizens live in little cabins and shanties on a permanent basis. For these unfortunates what for the privileged minority is a country home—as opposed to a city home—is their primary residence. For them, the distinction between country and city home does not exist; indeed this is their only residence. The dacha belonging to Tanya's family was a combination of the two, for her, NI, and her sister it was a dacha in the true sense of the word; they visited only on a sporadic basis—for occasional weekends in the spring, summer, and early fall. For Tanya's maternal grandparents, it was their primary residence. For Tanya's mother it was both—she lived there full time during the early spring, summer, and fall, and in Moscow in the winter, making occasional weekend trips to check up on her parents and assist them in any way necessary.

For Tanya, the family dacha was an object of distaste and annoyance rather than enjoyment. It was small, dilapidated, had no running water, and had a constant and unpleasant odor emanating from the nearby shed which sheltered the half-dozen or so goats her grandfather kept. There were chickens continually milling about, squawking their heads off, and pecking away to their heart's content. There were also a few malicious cats that were kept mainly for their rodent-hunting capabilities. Everything was covered with an abundant layer of dust, and this was particularly repugnant to someone who was as dedicated to cleanliness as Tanya was. But probably the main reason she disliked the dacha was that, instead of a place of needed rest on a rare day off it became a locus for hard physical work. Since everyone there worked pretty much from sunup to sundown, Tanya had also to draw and carry water from a well not too distant, irrigate the extensive vegetable garden, help in the harvest, put up preserves, and participate in the general upkeep of the building and grounds.

Despite her dislike of the place, however, after I had been seeing Tanya on a regular basis for quite some time and after I had grown into the good graces of her parents, she decided that it was time for me to come visit her family at the dacha. It transpired that her father had been putting on a bit of pressure to have me come spend a day with the entire family. Tanya and I demurred pointing out that my visa did not permit any unauthorized travel outside Moscow city limits. NI—who made it his business to know about such things—answered Tanya's plaint by stating that a foreign visa defined city limits as twenty-five kilometers from the center of the city. He further advised (rather conveniently, it seemed to me) that their dacha was located exactly twenty-five kilometers from the center of Moscow, and therefore it was permissible for me to travel there. So, we picked a Saturday and determined to spend the day there hoping that the weather would cooperate.

Galya and her husband, Seriozha, agreed to join us—which made the entire trip much more pleasant to anticipate. Without a car, the only way to the dacha was to take the subway to the *electrichka*—the electric train network that served so many commuters in and around any major urban center—then bounce and be jostled around for forty-fifty minutes to cover some twenty or so of the twenty-five kilometers to get there. The train ride was always a most disagreeable experience requiring as it did nearly an hour's worth of sitting on an uncomfortable wooden bench surrounded by a host of unwashed and malodorous bodies. After exiting the train, one had to trudge another 4-5 kilometers by foot since there was no public transportation in the area. I was fortunate enough that the first few times I visited the dacha I was offered a ride each time. I only learned later what a chore it was to get there without access to a private vehicle. I also gained great respect for Tanya's mother, for she almost invariably traveled by public transport—so deep was her dedication to her parents who lived permanently at the dacha.

So on the designated day Galya and Seriozha picked us up in their little Soviet style car and the four of us set off for the dacha. While on the way, I asked Tanya where the dacha had come from and received in response a generous dose of her family history. Because NI had been a very highly decorated war hero, he was eligible to receive a modest piece of land in one of the forests encircling Moscow as an expression of the government's gratitude for his sacrifices. His cost was purely symbolic—a pittance, in fact, for about three-quarters of an acre just twenty-five kilometers from the center of a huge urban mass. Since socialism under Soviet rule did not allow property ownership, NI was given a ninety-nine-year lease that endowed him with exclusive use of the property.

At about this time, Tanya's maternal grandmother was diagnosed with a weak heart, which was aggravated by the very hot weather of the village where she and her husband resided. They had lived their entire lives up to this point in the Kuban. The Kuban is an enormous area in southern Russia mostly noted for its Cossack traditions of pre-Soviet times and its agriculture both before and since. Because of the tremendous heat there which local doctors felt aggravated her condition, they advised her to move to a cooler climate. So Tanya's mother sent for her parents and arranged for them to reestablish themselves in Moscow. It would be difficult to imagine a greater change in people's lives: from a small, slow-moving village in southern USSR, living like peasants to a shared apartment in the biggest and most populous, noisy and polluted city in the country. It did not take long before they found the big city atmosphere so distasteful that they insisted on leaving. Finding an apartment for themselves in the overcrowded Moscow of that time was simply an impossibility, so sharing with Tanya's parents was the best they could do.

The Family Dacha

Tanya's mother despaired over her parents moving back south, so tried in every way she could to establish living accommodations for them that would be more acceptable than living in an overcrowded apartment in the center of Moscow. Since by this time the land had been given over to Tanya's father, her mother began to toil day and night until she had constructed a small shed on the property. As soon as she had completed a structure that could protect her parents, she moved them out of the city. They then began—the three of them plus one paid helper—the laborious job of building a cabin that would become her parents' permanent residence, and so was born Tanya's family dacha.

We drove almost straight west for about half an hour then got off the relatively well-maintained asphalt road. The next ten minutes were spent bumping and bouncing in a truly teeth-jarring ride over the most deeply rutted back road I have ever ridden on. To say that we scraped bottom almost continuously would be an understatement. It was a wonder that we had any undercarriage left to the car. Mercifully, we came down one terrible little alleyway then turned left at another. Looking through the front window, I saw blessed relief in the form of a fence that clearly bisected our roadway another hundred meters further—we had no option but to stop, ergo, we must be near our destination.

We left the car, carrying various food items, and headed for what we could discern as a wooden structure on the other side of the fence. We entered the territory through a gap in the rickety barrier that represented an open gate much in need of repair. It had been explained to me that the dacha had been built essentially by Tanya's relatives, so I was not expecting a mansion or anything else very elaborate. But what met my gaze was a bit disconcerting and not a little depressing. The entire shanty was painted green but obviously done at various times so that there were several different tones and shades. There was not a single straight line in the wooden structure—either vertical or horizontal. The construction was made up of many shapes and forms, no two of them alike. Clearly the dacha was built piece by piece, added onto when convenient or necessary, and in whatever direction seemed appropriate at the time. Some of the enclosures were roughly analogous to big boxes, others had quasi-octagonal shapes, still others had some square, some rounded edges. They were like gigantic children's' building blocks of various sizes and shapes designed and put together in a totally haphazard manner.

Forty steps further on to the immediate right stood a ramshackle shed which I later discovered housed the animal stock of the dacha: mostly goats and chickens. The narrow section between the fence on the right and the dacha on the left was probably about fifteen to eighteen feet of unusable border, fringed by trees and in constant shade. Around the house to the right was a surprisingly large field that stretched some sixty feet back to the left and another forty feet straight ahead to the fence on the opposite side from where we entered. This area was obviously very well-tended and was neatly divided into ranks and rows of tomatoes, strawberries, scallions, onions, garlic, and potatoes. Near the fence stood the family's alternative to indoor plumbing—an outhouse complete with tiny window cut out at the top of the entry door. The right side of the property sloped gradually down to a pond situated at the extreme lower end of their land. On this slope were a variety of fruit trees and a few berry bushes. A worn path led down to a spot skirting the edge of the pond. All in all the property was probably three-quarters of an acre with every available square foot of land under cultivation. The fence carried all the way around the periphery of the plot from one side of the pond to the other.

Directly opposite the goat shed was a tiny dilapidated porch accessed by a small staircase. We covered the forty paces and ascended the half-dozen steps, which sagged under our weight to an alarming degree. This was the entrance to the dacha proper. From the porch, we found ourselves in a miniscule vestibule, which was remarkable only for its darkness and somewhat disturbing odor. Directly past this was a tiny hallway that separated the structure; on one side a bedroom and kitchen (with as yet invisible root cellar), on the other another bedroom and sitting room/dining room. Here the odor I had detected in the vestibule became more pronounced. It was clearly the residue of decades of cooking and preserving with only a modicum of cleaning and scouring. Since there was only a pail of water with which to wash, bathing was an activity that was not considered very popular or necessary. There was probably some olfactory spillover from the goat shed as well. The other thing I immediately noticed was the heat; it was many degrees warmer than needed for comfortable indoor living.

Acquaintance with Tanya's Grandparents

We were ushered into the sitting room where we soon met Tanya's grandparents. Her mother made the introductions: first to a short but obviously very robust woman in her early eighties, then to a wizened old man in his mid-eighties. Grandmother had manifold wrinkles all across her forehead, around her eyes, and down her cheeks. She was permanently stooped over from decades of physical labor and moved slowly as if it was a chore to move abruptly or energetically. She had on several layers of clothing despite the excessive warmth of the room. On top of her head, she wore a kerchief which Americans invariably refer to as a "babushka" but which actually signifies grandmother or granny—that is, the person wearing the kerchief. In the years that followed and the many dozens of times I visited the dacha, I do not remember ever seeing her without her kerchief, occasionally accompanied by a shawl as well. She was rather short, probably measuring only a little over five feet tall. But weak she was not; stout and sturdy, she was clearly the vigorous product of regular and continuous physical labor and the natural elements.

Grandfather was no more than an inch taller than his spouse but was as thin as she was thickset. He was a real lightweight, probably no more than 120 pounds, but appeared wiry and tough and held himself as erect as a post. He, too, was dressed warmly as if preparing to go out-of-doors into the much cooler temperature. His lean face was also crisscrossed with a mass of wrinkles; whereas, grandmother's eyes were bright and clear his appeared dim and small, hidden as they were behind a pair of lenses that looked as thick as the legendary bottoms of coke bottles. His tiny head was perched atop a skinny neck, another locus of multiple wrinkles. He had very sparse hair that was rather long, white, and thin and tended to stick out in all directions. His nose was quite prominent as were his cheekbones. When we shook hands, I noticed that he was missing a finger on his right hand. His only words to me were, "So, you're the American." I indicated that I was and that was the last word I heard from him until he made a toast at dinnertime.

The next couple hours were spent with Tanya's mother and grandmother in the kitchen, grandfather in some undisclosed location, the rest of us either strolling in the nearby forests or visiting with one another in the sitting room of the dacha. Presently the women began bringing in food until the large table was abundantly covered by an assortment of plates, bowls, platters, and bottles. Everyone was invited to sit down according to some arrangement that only mother and grandmother understood. Grandfather was placed in the exact middle of the table. No sooner had we taken our seats than he was poured a glass of vodka. Whereas everyone else, except the two older women—who never drank any kind of spirits—had a standard shot glass in front of them, grandfather had a tapered affair with a small circumference at the bottom and wider opening at the top. His receptacle was crystal (whereas ours were made of glass) and about fifty percent taller than the rest. Its capacity was about one-and-a-half times that of the regular shot glasses. When all those who intended to partake of the vodka had been poured a shot, grandfather—as was appropriate for the eldest male in the room—arose from his chair, held out his glass and pronounced the first toast. Looking right at Tanya, he intoned with great solemnity, "Congratulations on marrying an American." After this totally unexpected, but mercifully brief speech, everyone took a sip of vodka and resumed their seats. I kept my attention on grandfather who, having also sat down, put on an unwitting exhibition that held me rapt. Instead of sipping some vodka like everyone else had done, he inclined his head backward and slowly tilted the glass so that the liquid poured straight down into his throat without coming in contact with lips, teeth or even, I believe, tongue. Then, keeping his head as far back as he apparently could, with the glass now in a perfectly perpendicular position, he thrust his tongue into the glass and thoroughly licked every single inside surface of it in order to remove any remaining molecule of moisture. I later learned that grandfather always drank out of the same glass and that he was allowed one shot of vodka every day and that he usually drank it with two to three raw eggs and a bowl of soup for breakfast. Sounds like a rather lethal combination but to whatever extent it contributed to his health, suffice to say that he lived to ninety-six, and was healthy as an ox to the very end of his life.

That was my first glimpse of grandfather, but I would have the opportunity to see him many times over the following years. Tanya and everyone else in her generation and the one that followed called him Ded so that is how I shall refer to him from now on since I was also encouraged to call him that. Ded is simply the short form of the word *dedushka,* which means grandfather in Russian. To say that Ded was a colorful individual would be an understatement. He grew up in the Kuban, a member of a small Cossack community. He was not a mercenary, however, like so many of his countrymen, in fact shunned any kind of physical conflict, and was content to keep herd and do a little farming.

Ded's main occupation every day was to take the goats out to pasture. On the occasional Saturday or Sunday when Tanya and I would travel to the dacha I would frequently search him out in the fields across the way. I would traverse the area between house and pond and make my way through the miniature gate between pond and fence left for the goats to access the fields beyond. Past the pond was a series of beautiful meadows that had apparently never been cultivated. The grass grew luxuriantly here and consequently was ideal for grazing the goats. This is where I usually found Ded. He would always be sitting under a tree somewhere with five or six goats browsing nearby. Sometimes he would be dozing, other times just staring out at nothing, most likely reminiscing. I enjoyed spending a little time with him coaxing him to tell me stories of times long past and a world I would never know but about which I had read extensively and which I found intriguing.

Ded's Background

Ded had been born and raised in the town of Stavropol. This was a center of a Cossack population like the Don area and the Kuban, but somewhat less known. He was from a Cossack family that was more accustomed to farming than military pursuits—the two main occupations of Cossacks. He was still a young man when he met Anna, the young and beautiful scion of a prominent and wealthy Ukrainian family. He made his living as a shoemaker and somehow had arranged with her family to do a number of repairs. He fell hopelessly in love with her notwithstanding her being from the upper class, he from a peasant background. After the revolution and subsequent civil war collectivism began to sweep through areas further removed from the centers of Moscow and St. Petersburg. The process was a brutal one and could entail loss of life as well as loss of all possessions. In a short period of time, her family found themselves in considerable danger, not only of losing their fortune, but also their freedom as well.

At this point, Ded made a proposition to Anna's family, which must have seemed extraordinary when first articulated. Despite the disparity in their social origins, he asked for her hand in marriage in return for which he would take her and move to another area of the country where she would be safe from the zealous enforcers of collectivization. After considering Ded's proposal and witnessing many of his friends and acquaintances losing their estates, their jewelry, and sometimes their freedom not to mention their lives, Anna's father acquiesced. He gave her a small pouch with some family treasures inside and sent the two on their way. A short time later, they settled in the Kuban region, having acquired a small plot of land in an isolated agricultural village in return for a few of Anna's jewels.

Their lives at first were rather quiet and unmemorable. Ded made and repaired footwear in the winter months and looked after his fruit trees in the other months. This activity kept him quite busy for the fruit trees required pruning and fertilizing in the spring, irrigating in the summer, and harvesting in the fall. Then he would put all the apricots and prunes on the roof of their cottage for drying. When the fruit was dried properly, he would take it to the market where he would barter for goods, he and Anna could not produce themselves, such as sugar, flour, and tea. Basically, though, they were almost self-sufficient, Anna's tasks were to look after the livestock, slaughter when the time was relevant, make cheese, and other milk-based products and do the cooking.

Zorka

One of the stories I most enjoyed hearing from Ded concerned one of Anna's cows. She had three: two of them were very calm and placid, followed orders and did as cows are supposed to do, in other words stand in a designated spot and chew their cud. The third was named Zorka and was as mean as a snake. Every day Anna would take the three cows to a central gathering spot where a herder collected the village cows, took them to a special grazing area and stood guard over them through the day. He would then bring them back in the evening at which time their owners would retrieve them and take them home. One day, Anna was indisposed and so could not look after the cows, so Ded was enjoined to take them to the spot where the herder picked them up. Everything went well, and Ded turned them over for the day. In the evening, he returned to fetch them home. On this occasion, however, Zorka became very recalcitrant, so Ded felt it necessary to tie her to a rope, which he wound around his hand to keep her under control. In order not to have to hold on to the rope, he knotted it around his right index finger. Halfway home Zorka spooked at something and started to run frenetically first in one direction, then in another. Ded was busy reining her in all the while cursing her in very colorful Ukrainian. But suddenly she turned and dashed straight toward him. At first rooted to the spot out of astonishment, a couple seconds later Ded moved sharply to the side and knelt down. However, Zorka kept going at full tilt and when she reached the end of her tether, Ded was in the awkward position of being turned only partway toward her and being on his knees. With an extra burst of energy, Zorka picked up her pace even further, pulling Ded all the way over on his back; nor did she stop or even slow down when she got to the end of the rope. Last thing Ded saw before the demented cow hove out of sight was the rope swinging and swaying crazily in the dust, his finger still entwined in it.

Imprisonment

The 1930s and 1940s were a very tumultuous time in the Soviet Union. Stalin was trying mightily to eliminate even the vestige of any opposition, and these efforts extended to all areas of the country—including the bucolic Kuban. He put into place the largest and cruelest secret service agency the world had known at that time. His henchmen refined the use of arrest, torture, mock trials, and officially sanctioned murder in order to control the unruly masses. Ded once told me the story of how he had got caught up in this web of danger and deceit. His sin against the state was the unwise recounting of an anecdote that was somewhat unflattering to Stalin himself. He was denounced, quickly picked up and, without even the sham of a trial, was convicted of state treason and sent to a north Siberian labor camp. Ded already had formed his own opinion of the Bolsheviks and their successors. As far as he was concerned, they were all corrupt thieves and liars and so his incarceration made him even more hostile to the Communists (which he always called Bolsheviks). For many years, he toiled within the confines of the prison camp and the forests nearby, for it was the job of his unhappy peers and himself to cut and trim trees and then roughly clean them for further processing elsewhere. Unlike many of the other prisoners, Ded did not overly suffer. He was by nature very slight and wiry of build, had worked at hard physical labor all his adult life, and had never been accustomed to frills of any kind. And so, though he did not thrive in the hostile environment, he also did not become increasingly exhausted, wither away, and give in to consumption or some other illness like so many of his peers. On the other hand, he did learn a whole new vocabulary of labor camp jargon and a host of colorful prison songs—which he later sang unceasingly at dinner after his quota of vodka—whether anyone wished to hear them or not.

He also learned to focus his distaste for the Bolsheviks on whatever administration was in power at that time and on their lower-level hirelings. Later in life, he would sit for hours at the kitchen table composing letters to local administration officials complaining about the price of bread, the poor service in providing water, gas, and other amenities, the corruption he saw everywhere around him. He would sit at the table for hours at a time, bent over with eyes merely inches from the paper, creating a script so tiny that if anyone ever read his letters, it would have required high-powered magnifiers to decipher. He would sometimes write ten or more pages vilifying the "Bolsheviks" whom he despised so much whether on the local or federal level. By this time, however—the 1960s through the 1980s—he was just considered a crank and no one paid any heed to his ramblings.

Saving Rubles

One of the stories I most enjoyed occurred not too long after Ded and Anna moved from the Kuban to Moscow because her doctor had advised that the hot temperatures of their homeland were debilitating to her health, and she should move to a more temperate clime. In preparation for the move, they sold off their livestock, their cottage, and the land itself, which they had been farming for so many years. For this, they received sufficient cash to repurchase other livestock after settling into the area near Moscow and still have a pretty substantial nest egg. This was before changes in the monetary policy, so the ruble value of the cash they had was worth only a tenth of what it would be after the serious devaluation; therefore, the physical bundle of money was ten times bulkier than it would have been later. Ded took the cash and rolled it up into as tight a cylinder as he could manage, tied several strings around it, and wrapped it in some old newspapers. He then hid it in a location known only to himself. From time to time, he would check on it until one day when he retrieved the roll he noted that it was considerably lighter and the wrap around the outside was tattered and chewed up. He quickly unwrapped it and discovered to his everlasting horror and dismay that over the months that he had not checked on his money the rats had feasted on the rubles. His and Anna's nest egg had indeed become a nest for the rats. They had been so efficient that they had eaten their way through parts of every single bill. The upshot was that no one—not a store, not an individual, not even a bank would accept any of the old script.

In the Pond

Ded lived a long life; indeed, he finally succumbed only after his ninety-sixth birthday, and this he did painlessly and peacefully in his bed and, as far as anyone knew, asleep. The year or so before he died he began to show signs of decline. Not that he became ill; on the contrary, he was in excellent health until the day he died. But from time to time he would skip a day of taking the goats out to graze or decide to forego the market, which required a two-mile trek. On one beautiful day, Tanya and I had visited for a few hours but needed to get back to Moscow for meetings I had with some arriving business people. Mother and grandmother were working in the garden; Ded set off for the meadows in his big floppy boots. We said our good-byes and made for the car. Just as we were exiting the dacha's territory through the gate, we heard a piercing cry. This was followed by a whole series of screams from both Tanya's mother and grandmother. We dropped what we were carrying and dashed back into the yard. The women had congregated on the slope toward the back of the property. As we approached, it became immediately clear what the cause of such great consternation was: Ded had somehow fallen into the pond. He was floundering badly, dragged down by his accursed boots. Sputtering and wheezing he was flailing about with both arms—which action was only propelling him further toward the middle of the pond. I ran to the water's edge and jumped in. In a couple moments, I managed to drag him close enough to the pond's perimeter for the others to grab hold as well. We all heaved and pulled until we extricated Ded. For the first few minutes, he just lay there gasping and spitting out foul water. Then he sat up, looked at his boot-clad feet and muttered, "You damned boots just about did me in that time!" Tanya and I cleaned me up as well as we could and got in the car for our interrupted return back to Moscow.

ANYA'S DEATH
AND AFTERMATH

Suddenly Anya—who had never eaten particularly well—lost her appetite completely. She became listless and started complaining of a general malaise, dizziness, and nausea. Tanya immediately took her to the doctor who performed a series of tests on her and recommended that other specialists examine Anya as well. After weeks of all kinds of poking, prodding, ex-raying, and drawing of blood the doctors were unanimous about one fact only—that she had an acute case of anemia. Next began an excruciating period of Tanya and Viktor performing Herculean efforts to get the girl to eat the doctors' recommended dietary foods while the child continued to resist almost everything. Her condition deteriorated even further, so her parents took her to yet another specialist who pronounced the most dreaded diagnosis imaginable—he thought she might have leukemia. He did hold out some hope; however, he advised that there were many treatments available, including chemotherapy—which at that time was still in comparatively early stages of usage.

During this particularly arduous time for Tanya, two other factors came into play that made her life even more painful and complicated. Viktor, who had studiously avoided any physical contact at all with her, began to beat her again. He also picked this time to begin an affair with a woman who lived on another floor in the same apartment complex. To make matters worse, the woman had been a friend of both of them for many years. Since Tanya and Viktor had been separated for a significant period of time by now—despite living in the same apartment—it was not a difficult or complicated next step to a divorce. The fact that Viktor wanted the divorce as much as Tanya made it rather easy to work out the details. It was particularly easy since Anya could live with the grandparents—thus no custody concerns—and they had virtually no assets to be divided. The divorce itself was somewhat anti-climactic. It required no more than their appearance before a magistrate, an explanation of why they could no longer live as husband and wife and making an application for a divorce certificate. And so ended an extremely cheerless and unhappy eight-year union.

The single positive aspect of Tanya and Viktor's relationship was Anya. The doctors continued their therapy—chemicals and radiation as well as continuous blood transfusions. Tanya was almost a perfect match for Anya and so constantly gave blood, sometimes so frequently as to be alarming. Also, the needles back then were not of very good quality; consequently Tanya's arms and legs would sometimes be a mass of purple bruises caused by the blunt needle points. In addition, doctors believed in the therapeutic value of certain foods such as pomegranate, black caviar, and raw calf's liver (however, since there was no calf meat available, this turned out to be steer liver). Unfortunately, Anya loathed liver, and there was not a pomegranate available in all of

Moscow—at least to anyone with less of a position than, say, a deputy minister. So Tanya tried wherever possible to get the caviar. This was, naturally, rather expensive; so Tanya was forced to supplement her regular—not so generous—income by doing some trading on the black market.

Every once in a while, Anya would show some serious progress and the doctors would triumphantly proclaim their programs to be successful. During these times of remission, Anya would usually move back to Tanya's parents' home where she could get full-time attention from her grandmother who had by now taken leave of absence from work. Tanya was now working the equivalent of two jobs, was eating sporadically at best, and had started losing a considerable amount of weight herself. But everyone in the family would be jubilant that Anya was significantly better, that perhaps this latest remission was actually the final cure that would solve all her medical problems.

Then, cruelly, she would suffer a setback and end up again in the oncological clinic. Each time she came out of remission, it seemed that she was worse than the time before. My boss, Saul, and I brought the most up-to-date medicines we could get in the United States, but these proved equally as ineffective as those she was getting locally. The poor child lost her hair and became bloated. Physically she was deteriorating fast, but mentally she was just as sharp as ever. She drew very clever pictures and read everything Tanya could get her hands on relating to Greek and Roman mythology. The cycle of in remission, out of remission lasted about a year and a half, and I believe that toward the end of this phase it became clear to Tanya that Anya's condition was not improving, but rather worsening. Her cancerous blood cell count increased significantly from one month to the next and she became even more listless than she had been. When she was not experiencing pain or being nauseous from the incessant intake of chemicals, drugs, and radiation, she would sleep for protracted periods of time.

During the lengthy period of time that Anya was sick, there was certainly no occasion for Tanya and me to consider or discuss any sort of permanent relationship. We simply took each day as it came, hoped for the best, and dealt with each crisis as it occurred. I tried to give her as much support and comfort as possible, knowing full well that it had to be miniscule in comparison to the pain and suffering she was experiencing. We saw each other as often as opportunities presented themselves. I was in Moscow in July of that year and was due to return in early September for several more weeks. I was, in fact, making every effort possible to visit Moscow as frequently as I could.

The original international airport—before the Soviets built the new one to handle the anticipated huge influx of air travelers expected for the 1980 Olympics—was tiny, primitive, and severely lacking in security. Incoming passengers had to go through passport control as a necessary first step. Then they would enter a hallway where, with any kind of luck, they would locate their luggage. At one side of the hall opposite the obsolete luggage carousels were several aisles created by placing tables end to end. After finding their baggage passengers would line up at these aisles for customs inspection. Just to the side of these aisles was an open area with nothing but a low railing to separate travelers from precustoms to post customs sections. And along this railing would gather as many friends and family members meeting passengers as could offer a small bribe to officials to let them enter an area that should have been shielded from everyone but passengers and bureaucrats.

In expectations of visiting Anya at the hospital, I had bought a large, soft animal figure that she should find very floppy and cozy to cuddle up against. I was carrying it in a bag that was a little small for the doll so that its head appeared to be looking out. When I cleared immigration and made my way into the next hall I immediately looked over at the railing, for Tanya always met me at the airport and invariably managed to get inside to greet me before I even went through customs. I saw her right away and hurried over. She saw the doll and started weeping. When we hugged each other in greeting, she whispered that the reason for her tears was because Anya had died three days previously. I had not known about it for I had had several days' worth of appointments in Europe on my way to Moscow and when Tanya notified my parents, they could not locate me to pass on the tragic news.

For the next few days, I tried to spend as much time as possible with Tanya. She was terribly broken up over Anya's death. Perversely, her parents and Viktor as well put a good deal of the blame for the tragedy on Tanya herself, irrationally equating her relationship with a hated foreigner with treachery toward her own daughter. This made Tanya—already inconsolable—extremely bitter at the enormous inequity and injustice of the situation. And so her boundless grief over the loss of her beloved daughter was exacerbated by the growing hostility of those others who had been closest to that same daughter. The following weeks and months were the most difficult Tanya had ever lived through—even worse than the lengthy period when Anya was actually ill. Because Tanya cared so deeply for me, I was the single refuge in an otherwise, hostile and angry environment.

However, in one of those outrageously ironic moments that sometimes occur on this earth, we began to realize that there was no longer any insurmountable obstacle to our getting married and starting a life together. While Anya was alive, and especially when she was sick, there could never have been any thought of Tanya and me marrying and her moving to the States to join me. However, now the calculus of her existence in Moscow had changed dramatically. Mind you, she still had important family ties, but they were no longer so powerful as to make such a move unthinkable. At first, tentatively, then with ever-greater frequency and seriousness, we discussed the idea of getting married. We accepted the dual facts that we had loved each other for many years by now and genuinely wanted to share our lives with one another. We had just not considered this a possibility before the tragedy of Anya's death.

THE HOTEL BERLIN

This corpus of memories would not be complete without a short description of the place we called home when we were in Moscow. It also played a significant role in some of the rather important events that followed Anya's passing. The particular hotel we stayed in—the Hotel Berlin—became for us our sleeping quarters, our office facilities, and the center for rare instances of entertainment. We ate virtually all our meals in the hotel restaurant, made and received almost all our telephone calls there, and, occasionally held meetings in our suite of rooms. It had a large bedroom and a somewhat luxurious bath, so this is where my supervisor stayed when we were in Moscow together, and where I stayed whenever he was not accompanying me. In a sense, it was something of a refuge for us; the suite was a warm and comfortable site in an otherwise often cold and inhospitable environment. Ultimately, the hotel became a major reason Tanya and I were able to evade some of the biggest impediments of Soviet bureaucracy and actually complete the marriage registration process during one of my visits there.

Through an agreement that was mutually advantageous to both our firm and the Hotel Berlin (and finally the state-wide organization Intourist and, ultimately, the Soviet government), we reserved and paid for a suite 365 days a year. Intourist was the equivalent of a FTO having monopoly rights for processing all foreigners into the Soviet Union and issuing all entry and travel documents. From the hotel's and Intourist's perspective, the deal guaranteed that this particular apartment would be occupied year round with concomitant revenue (in hard currency), and at the same time ensured at least one available accommodation for our company any time we chose—an essential requisite to getting a Soviet visa. Indeed, there were many occasions when we were able to secure a visa in record time rather than wait the endless weeks that, otherwise, most likely would have been required while limited hotel space freed up for one or another of us.

The hotel building itself went back a long ways. It was built in the early part of the twentieth century and was originally called "the Savoy." A fairly modest affair standing most of the way down a small side street in the middle of Moscow, it was a bit off the beaten path and not very well known to most foreigners. It was located opposite the so-called Children's World, a store devoted to the sale of clothing, accessories, and toys for young people from babies to teenagers. There were only three buildings on the entire street—Children's World taking up the whole block on the one side and a large ministerial building with our more modest edifice on the opposite side. The Berlin was gray on the outside thus blending in well with the rest of Moscow's gray buildings. Yet there was something a bit different about it; it seemed to exude a certain class that Stalinesque and Krushchevian structures did not have. It was small, but kind of elegant in the seedy sort of way that a down-on-his luck nobleman might appear.

Two massive wooden doors, one of which—in typical Soviet fashion—was always closed and locked, formed the main entrance into the building. Upon entering, one would find himself in a large hallway extending from right to left. Across the hall to the right was the building's only elevator and directly opposite this mechanism was an open cloakroom. To the left near the stairway leading to the upper reaches of the building was a very imposing, larger-than-life, stuffed bear that stood on a three-foot pedestal, thus towering over even the tallest visitor. The very first thing to be seen upon entering the hotel was this ubiquitous symbol of the hale and hearty Russian. Further to the left was a small kiosk devoted to the sale of Soviet propaganda in the form of little souvenirs, brochures, postcards, city maps, and the like. Between the kiosk and the bear was a counter dedicated to "Intourist" services. During the daytime, visitors could request tickets for the circus (international talent of the highest order) or tours of the Kremlin (the political center of the Soviet Union), the Tretiakov Gallery (an absolutely mind-numbing display of artistic treasures), Zagorsk (the heart of Russian Orthodoxy) or other fascinating sites. This was also where guests requested automobiles to be chauffeured around the impossibly convoluted streets of Moscow. Other services included tours to other Soviet cities, tickets to the theater, reservations for train or plane, and so forth.

Rita

Directly opposite the entrance was a staircase of twelve or fifteen steps that bifurcated at the top. To the right, a massively wide and elaborate staircase continued up to the first through fifth floors—the guests' havens. Straight ahead was an office devoted to the hotel administration. This was the lair of a half-dozen or so women who held sway over the fates of hundreds of guests during the course of the year. Thankfully, the chief administrator was a woman of rare (in those Soviet times) kindness and consideration who cared more about her foreign charges than fulfilling her quota. Her name was Rita (short for Margarita), and she was always the second person we greeted whenever visiting Moscow. Rita was an enormous woman with fold upon fold of flesh overlapping each other down her neck and arms and, one would imagine, down the rest of her as well. She wore spectacles but one could almost always see the twinkle in her eyes. She was the warmest bureaucrat I ever met in the old Soviet days. This is not to say she did not run a tight ship. On the contrary, she administered the most efficient hotel facility in Moscow. Her coworkers actually tried to fulfill their duties since she was so liked and respected and seemed even to enjoy their work environment.

Zhenya

I mentioned that Rita was usually the second person we acknowledged when arriving at the hotel—which brings us to the first person we greeted when coming to town. The individual who invariably met us when we entered the Hotel Berlin (when he was on shift) was a gentleman named Zhenya. Actually, Zhenya was not much of a gentleman; he was more of an old war-horse. He was not tall—about five foot nine, was spare, maybe one hundred and fifty pounds, had sparse gray hair, and a face that seemed chiseled out of sandstone. Chin and cheekbones composed of sharp planes and angles, cunning eyes that glittered like tiny black marbles and the most imposing four gold teeth set prominently on top and squarely in the front of his mouth. At some stage in his life, Zhenya had apparently determined that these gold teeth were his most attractive feature for he smiled at every possible occasion and frequently when there was no reason whatsoever to smile. The smile itself was something rather fierce for he spread his lips so widely that virtually all his teeth were visible.

Every time I entered the hotel after a trip back to the States, Zhenya would rush over, wrap his arms around me, and shower my cheeks with a dozen kisses. Once, he was reprimanded by the in-house KGB man, who complained that such a warm and effusive greeting of an American was unseemly. Whereupon Zhenya immediately retorted that it was, after all, the Americans who sent boots to the distressed front-line Soviet soldiers freezing in muddy trenches with their bare feet during the war with Germany. Zhenya never forgot that he was one of the fortunate recipients of this largesse. And since we invariably brought gifts for him (alcohol of some sort—usually whiskey that he had no access to) and his family (trinkets of various kinds) he continued to be a grateful recipient of charitable American contributions.

After we checked in, we would return to the ground level where Zhenya would grab a piece of luggage and usher us over to the lift. Now this was an unforgettable machine. Four very skinny people carrying nothing larger than a fountain pen could have fit in at one time—providing they did not all inhale at once. If one suitcase and I were in the elevator, Zhenya could just manage to fit himself in as well. Invariably he would immediately turn toward me and start asking about the latest news about home, family, and other colleagues. He had a habit of opening his mouth wide when talking and sort of exhaling while doing so. Zhenya *loved* garlic. In fact, the only thing in the world he might have preferred over garlic was vodka. His talking and exhaling while located only a foot away in a very confined space had a simply devastating effect on me. The elevator clanked and rattled away as it rose up the shaft as if human slaves were pulling it up hand over hand with a chain. Even though there were only five floors in the hotel, it seemed to take forever to get to the top. In the meantime, the effects of the garlic fumes practically put me in a state of stupefaction. I would be almost reeling by the time we reached our destination. And of course, the glitter and gleam reflected from the overhead light off Zhenya's gold teeth helped complete the feeling of disorientation.

There were not a lot of rooms, and they were absolutely unlike more modern hotel accommodations—each room was different from all the rest in size, shape, and accouterments. There were only five stories with about eighteen or twenty rooms on each. The one we rented on a full-time basis was number 516, a lavish eighteenth century affair that was actually a suite made up of three rooms. As you entered the suite there was a great room, very large, somewhat formal, with polished hardwood floor under plush throw rugs, expensive draperies (actually made of a beautiful fabric that our company had donated to the hotel), ornate seven teenth century furniture, and high ceilings adorned with gilt-edged sculptures around the entire perimeter.

The second room was a very spacious bedroom with more seventeenth-century furniture including a bed expansive enough to accommodate four large adults easily. The third room was an enormous bathroom complete with a tub that could fit half the bed's capacity with room to spare. Communist austerity it was not.

This was the center of our activity when we were in Moscow. It's where we lived, frequently ate breakfast, prepared for work, and made all our phone calls to set up appointments, arrange for transfer of promotional materials and do whatever negotiating did not require face-to-face encounters. We also did a small amount of entertaining there when the group was manageable and a full-fledged dinner was not necessary. When I was alone in Moscow, it was where I would wait until Tanya was free so we could meet after my obligations were discharged. She would call me from a little phone booth across the street near the "Children's World." The calling station was located conveniently just across the street from the hotel so that I could see her if I looked out the corner window of our suite.

The Restaurant

I said small amount of entertaining since virtually all the corporate entertaining we did was in the hotel's restaurant. This facility at the Hotel Berlin was on the ground level but on the opposite side of the building from the main hotel entryway. Access for patrons to the restaurant was twofold. Around the corner from the front entrance was a doorway with small vestibule that gave on to the smaller section of the L-shaped facility, the lower right-hand tip. The other entrance was from a staircase that descended from a point next to the hotel administration office. That point of entry was for hotel guests only and was at the extreme top end of the L. Tables with the purest white coverings were placed at discreet intervals along the two lengths of the L, providing enough seating facilities to accommodate probably 120 patrons. Along one side of the hall were enormous windows where one could watch the pedestrian traffic when the drapes were open. The other wall held a series of dramatic mirrors framed on all sides with beautiful gilt sculptures. The ceiling was adorned with exquisite crystal chandeliers and the corners where walls and ceiling met sported complex and ornate sculptures covered with gilt like the mirrors.

Tucked away in an expanded area at the outside point where the long and short prongs of the L converged was a cozy little niche where an old-fashioned band was ensconced most evenings. Since most modern music was considered suspect by party bureaucrats and purveyors of music could be held accountable for playing anything even remotely decadent, the band at the Hotel Berlin restaurant tended to stick to safer music like traditional Soviet tunes and western music of the 1940s era. This, then, was the fare most evenings at the Berlin Restaurant. However, safe music could also be played with abandon and zest. Once the band cranked it up, there was usually such a din that you could not hear your next-door neighbor speak. When my boss and I came down for a late dinner, we invariably requested a table as far away from the band as possible. This way it was possible to carry on a conversation and still enjoy watching the antics of other patrons at the far end of the hall.

Sergei Sergeevich

Whereas Rita was the unassailable queen of the hotel, the entire restaurant facility was under the jurisdiction of a gentleman we knew only as Sergei Sergeevich. SS, as I will call him, presided over his little domain like a king with absolute power. He was small—probably no more than five feet seven tall, on the thin side, wizened and wrinkled. He had a sharp nose, high cheekbones, a grayish complexion, and coal-black greasy hair that he combed straight to the back of his head. It gave the impression of a gleaming, inky, greasy mass spread evenly over his scalp. As a match for his hair, he invariably wore a severe black suit, white shirt, and black tie. He had a permanent scowl on his face and if you were allowed one word to describe him, probably the most apt would be dour. SS's mouth sagged, and he always looked as if he expected some imminent terrible tragedy.

Where the two sides of the restaurant's L intersected, exactly across from where the band played, was a fishpond with fountain. Carp would usually inhabit this miniature artificial lake, and one of the delicacies of the house was considered a fish fresh from the pond, pan-fried, and served with various herbs and spices and a healthy dollop of potatoes. If a patron so desired, he could request fish from the menu—considered a real delicacy since fresh fish were something of a scarcity in Moscow. Since this was considered an entrée of considerable sophistication, SS invariably got involved. The waiter who had received the order would advise SS who would then personally accompany the customer to the pond and assist him in selecting his meal. This was always done with a good deal of solemnity and ceremony. With great aplomb, SS would then motion to a lowly waiter standing in attendance who would take a net and secure the prize.

Since there was a serious dearth of good restaurants in Moscow at the time I am describing and since there was a never-ending supply of wannabe restaurant patrons, the few acceptable facilities were always full. A good restaurant would always have a number of hopefuls milling about outside the entryway with vague ideas that just maybe they could somehow be admitted. Indeed, the window of the street-door entrance to the restaurant was almost always adorned with a sign that stated bluntly, "No Places Available." And this, of course, explains why being a maître d' at a good establishment was considered an excellent and lucrative posting. A typical honorarium for securing a reservation could be in the ten-ruble range and that for gaining admittance later when all the tables were occupied could easily be double that. To put this into perspective, the average Soviet salary back then was 100-120 rubles a month.

Restaurant Protocol

And so it was that SS was probably one of the wealthier of Moscow's nonpolitical entities. His base salary was certainly not very extraordinary, but the various gifts and contributions he garnered during the course of a typical evening were sufficient to put him in the top categories of revenue earners. Since the revelers were intent only on having a good time, they did not pay much attention to what it cost them. In general, Russians tend to enjoy themselves in a rather extravagant style. When they were partying, they were frequently flamboyant to the extreme. So a generous gift to the maître d' only enhanced the night's fun by ensuring good food and good service.

When Russians went out for an evening's entertainment, they wanted to get their money's worth. And they tended not to stint. There were not many choices available. One could go to the opera or ballet, to the circus, or to the restaurant. When one went to the restaurant, it was for the entire evening and usually to celebrate a special event such as a birthday, a promotion, International Ladies' Day, and so forth. In Soviet restaurants at the time, there was absolutely no table turnover. A group would arrive early in the evening and stay until the establishment was closed. During that period of time that frequently lasted six hours or more, they would consume prodigious amounts of food and drink.

As an accompaniment to the food, drink, and general merriment, the band would strike up music that would challenge the eardrums. To say that the music was usually spirited would be a staggering understatement; it was usually infectious, sometimes deafening and frequently compelling, and Russians on their night out loved to dance. The spectacle that would usually greet our eyes when we looked out at the dance floor was multiple bodies bouncing, prancing, and sometimes leaping, always stomping—arms flailing, all moving parts doing just that—moving. Sometimes you would get the impression of melodic noise almost unbearable in its decibel intensity, a mass of cavorting, sweating bodies frenetically moving to some rhythm known only to themselves. What they lacked in grace, they more than made up for in enthusiasm and exuberance. The very floor would seem to vibrate in time to their gyrations. But they were having such a good time!

Occasionally, the pond I earlier described would serve as a venue slightly different from simply selecting a fish for dinner. I remember one evening when a group of Japanese businessmen was gathered around a table having a very boisterous time. I guessed that they had successfully negotiated a substantial contract that day with a Soviet trade organization. Someone had taught them how to quaff vodka Russian style, that is, pop down a shot of the fiery liquid straight followed by a pickle, black bread, or herring. For Russians, this was a typical way of spending the evening—multiple shots of alcohol mixed with enormous quantities of rich food interspersed with frenetic bouts of dancing. The Japanese, however, were ill equipped for such exertion. After a couple hours of what was for them very strenuous activity, they started getting rather rambunctious. I noticed that several of them had adopted the perfectly acceptable local practice of inviting Russian women to dance—even though they were not at all acquainted.

Three or four of them were inviting luscious young Russian women to dance with them. Despite the fact that they were clearly unaccustomed to exercising with such feverish spirit, they were wildly flailing their arms about, bounding, and cavorting with total abandon. It was amusing to observe them, for the Russian women were young, tall, statuesque, and obviously abundantly energetic. Additionally, they were very fair, with blonde hair and classic Slavic good looks. The contrast could not have been more acute—the men were all middle-aged, out of shape, somewhat corpulent, and significantly shorter than their partners. Whereas the Russian women were graceful and athletic, the Japanese businessmen were rather clumsy and ungainly.

One couple particularly stood out. The Asian businessman was a short little guy, a bit overweight, of dark complexion, but clearly showing the effects of his strenuous drinking activity. His face was blotched with red spots, his suit showed obvious sweat stains, and he was breathing with pronounced difficulty. But I had to give him points for gaminess; he was bouncing and leaping and frolicking almost as if he were responding to some kind of mortal challenge to his manhood. His partner was a tall willowy and fair young woman who danced with grace and polish and, seemingly, without effort. Their movements were a total contrast to one another—his clumsiness a complete mismatch to her charm and elegance. I suppose it was inevitable. At one point, he became particularly rowdy and, being in the immediate vicinity of the fishpond at the very moment when he was giving his every effort to an improbably complicated dance maneuver, tumbled in with a loud cry and a splash. I suspect I will never forget the moment when he emerged from the pond dripping wet, a water lily draped over one shoulder and spectacles hanging from a single frame from one ear. In typical Russian fashion, everyone gave a hearty round of applause and the band carried on as if this were a nightly occurrence and a perfectly acceptable one at that.

I have spent a few moments describing the Hotel Berlin because it was an integral part of our life in Moscow and the center of so much of our non-working activity. It also became a small but very important part of our wedding plans since it played a crucial role in avoiding one bureaucratic obstacle that could have indefinitely delayed our matrimonial agenda.

GETTING MARRIED

Since most domestic ties had been severed by now, Tanya and I decided to get married. There was a ton of paperwork to plough through, but it was not at all an unheard-of thing for a foreigner and a Soviet citizen to marry. This is not to say that it was a frequent occurrence either. It was rare enough that people took notice. By this time, we had been seeing each other every trip I made to Moscow as often as possible. These trips spanned a period of nearly five years and were so frequent that no more than two months ever went by without my visiting Moscow on business. The year we determined to get married was a very difficult one for Tanya. She lost her job, her husband, and her daughter.

Since the relationship between Tanya and Viktor had long ago deteriorated to the point where they found it difficult to even converse about Anya and since Viktor had openly been carrying on an affair with one of their neighbors, Anya's death brought about the severing of whatever ties had remained, and they formalized the situation through divorce. At about this time, certain key personnel at Tractoroexport, realizing that Tanya was seeing a foreigner on a regular basis, ensured that she was fired without any possibility of reinstatement. Shortly afterward she was offered—through contacts—a position in another organization. The new job amounted to a significant downgrading in Tanya's professional life in that it did not require nor, indeed, even allow any decision-making or initiative. It was basically a paper-shuffling situation, a bureaucrat's dream. After a short time, pressure from within the organization put an end to this employment as well; so Tanya was left without any work or even the possibility of securing any.

We set about collecting the various papers necessary for the typical Soviet wedding, and the many additional ones necessary when the marriage involved a foreigner. A great deal of paperwork had to be generated, and it turned out that the task of determining precisely what papers, documents, and certificates were required was almost as serious a challenge as the collection of the documents themselves. The task was a daunting one indeed, for the required documents were copious and varied. Papers I was forced to amass, for example, originated in bureaucracies in my hometown, city, county, state, church, Washington, DC, and the US Embassy in Moscow.

The Palace of Weddings

When Tanya and I had secured all the various documents, papers, certificates, attestations, and the like that were necessary to make a wedding application plus stamps, signatures, and seals—approximately six months of bureaucratic haggling—we went to the central Palace of Weddings to request an appointment to register. This was the only place in Moscow where a foreigner could receive authorization to get married, and the only organization from which his marriage would be officially recognized, an essential element in Tanya's hoped-for emigration process. The registration itself was a fairly simple procedure that basically involved putting a stamp into the passports of the couple getting married, and filling in the blanks such as name, date, and location of the civil ceremony. The stamp and filled-in information signified the official marriage of the couple. The only real complexity was in amassing all the documents essential for a *foreigner* to participate. After collecting all the paperwork, it was only necessary to wait for official review of all records and certification that all were in order. Then one could apply for a confirmed date and time for the registration event itself.

We arrived at the Palace of Weddings and immediately requested a meeting with the director. In time, we were invited into a cavernous office, sparsely furnished with high ceilings and walls that seemed to rise far in the distance. An intimidating scene! The director was an imposing woman of forty-five or so, very officious and, it transpired, rather pompous. She sat at a huge desk bare of everything except a telephone and a thick appointment book. Without introducing herself, she curtly invited us to take seats at a tiny little table appended to the center of her massive desk opposite where she herself was ensconced. She asked for all our documents and then perused them for some time in silence while Tanya and I sat and anxiously waited. While we fidgeted, she leafed through our papers never asking a single question to clarify the information she was digesting. After a time, she notified us that we should move to the hallway in front of her office and take seats there while waiting to be summoned by "an associate." At the end of that meeting, we should return to her office.

The Vetting Process

We took the seats pointed out to us and began what later seemed to be an interminable wait. An hour went by, then another, then yet another. No one appeared. Midday arrived, still later it began to darken outside. Tanya had already gone to the director's office to determine whether we were waiting in vain or whether her associate was really coming. She repeatedly advised us to keep waiting and be patient. Finally, a gentleman in uniform appeared and entered the director's office. In a few moments, he exited, approached us, and asked us to confirm our surnames. When we gave them, he invited us to join him in his office at the other end of the hall.

We entered a small, but elegantly furnished room with modern furniture and bright lights. I also remember that it was warm—a real rarity at this time of the year in the rest of official Moscow. He was dressed in an exquisite military uniform that had clearly been tailored specifically for him. He had obviously served somewhere in the west and, I suspected, in a rather high position. He wore ribbons and medals whose significance I could only guess at; they were very impressive and hinted at an outstanding and officially recognized service in his career. He was probably in his fifties, but looked no more than forty-two. To say that he was fit would be a vast understatement. He motioned us to the seats in front of his desk. The chairs in the director's office were plain wooden straight-backed affairs; these were plush and comfortable leather armchairs.

He then began to act in a manner most startling to me. In a soft and cultured voice, he questioned whether we were really serious about our intention to marry, whether we were aware of the difficulties that might confound people of such vastly differing cultures and if Tanya realized how complicated she might make her family situation if she married a foreigner, especially an American. We answered that we were aware of the potential problems but that we had known each other for nearly five years and so were pretty clear about each other's intentions. We pointed out that we were not youngsters befuddled by the confusion of first love, but mature individuals who had, in fact, both experienced lengthy if rather unhappy unions earlier in life. Tanya explained that her family's situation could not be terribly compromised since her father—a highly decorated officer in the Red Army—had retired several years ago. She mentioned that there could not be any other familial impediments for her daughter had recently passed away, and she and her husband had divorced over a year ago. Our host then totally astounded us. He stated that since our movements had been regularly monitored for nearly five years and since we had obviously never attempted to hide anything from the authorities, the dossier created for us had by now grown to a thickness of almost ten inches, and it appeared they knew enough about us to realize that our marriage posed no particular threat to the Soviet state. He then cordially dismissed us advising that we had completed all formalities that concerned his office. He suggested that we return immediately to the director's office since it was getting late and wished us good luck. We thanked him profusely and promptly returned to the director's office. On the way, I whispered the question to Tanya, "Who was that?" she responded that he was, of course, the official KGB representative.

As I mentioned elsewhere, hotel space in Moscow was a chronic problem. There were only a limited number of facilities that were considered respectable enough to house western business people. Since business was expanding rather rapidly, the problem was greatly exacerbated due to the mounting numbers of would-be visitors. It resulted in waiting weeks or even longer to receive visas, for it was an absolute requirement that every visa had to be accompanied by a corresponding reserved hotel room.

The director reviewed the registration list and advised us that the first available open slot was December 19. She then asked how long before my visa expired. When I notified her that it was up on December 14, she pleasantly asked if I could extend until December 20, knowing full well that it was most likely impossible. However, what she did not know was that I had access to a room in the Hotel Berlin on a continuous basis. I said that I would make every effort to get my visa extended and, in the meantime, could she please keep the December 19 date reserved for us. She complied, entered our names and passport data in her appointment book and bid us good-bye, while Tanya and I rushed off to the Berlin. She was likely amused and content that this action most probably thwarted a foreigner's intention to marry a Russian girl.

We immediately went to the service bureau where, luckily, Rita, the manager, was on duty. She was a very hardworking and conscientious young woman who actually juggled things well enough to discharge all the duties of a hotel director in an enormously complex bureaucracy and yet remain a real human and caring individual. She actually treated hotel guests like real people and not like homeless vagabonds whose temporary residence was to be suffered with sometimes ill-concealed malice, then good riddance to them. I had known Rita ever since first staying at the hotel over four years before. She was a very amiable woman, had a very quick and dry wit, and knew every customer by name. She smiled rarely, but there was always a warm glow in her eyes. Rita had been a widow for many years and was raising a single daughter. There was a benevolent sadness about her, but perhaps that contributed to her being more kindhearted and generous than most bureaucrats. Tanya frequently visited me in the hotel and would always take the time to greet Rita and visit with her for a few minutes. I also dropped in to see her every day she was on duty. I always brought her a small souvenir of some kind from the States, and she appreciated this for it signified thoughtfulness, not some small-scale bribery. Consequently, we had a pretty good relationship.

When Tanya and I arrived at the Berlin after leaving the Palace of Weddings, we immediately explained our situation to Rita. My visa was up on December 14, and the earliest date we could have the marriage ceremony was December 19. Could she please manage to get my visa extended on the basis of having a hotel room? She got one of those expressions on her face that was very close to a wink when she replied that she would look into it and see what she might be able to do for us. I surrendered my visa that was due to expire shortly and set my fingers in a quasi-permanently crossed position. In fact, Rita called me in a couple days with the good news that my visa had been extended to December 20. Tanya immediately contacted the Palace of Weddings' director and confirmed our registration reservation for December 19. A potentially huge bureaucratic problem was resolved at this moment since our failure to complete the registration process on Dec. 19 might have resulted in indefinite delays in confirming a new registration date.

Celebrating the Wedding

Next step was to arrange witnesses for the ceremony. Because of the controversial nature of the wedding Galya and Seriozha both opted out of direct participation in the event. Tanya and I discussed the situation at length and determined that the people who had demonstrated the most loyalty and support to us during those many difficult years were Kolya and his wife, Galya. So we decided that they should be invited to act as our witnesses. This almost turned out to be a catastrophe. On the designated day, we arrived at the Palace of Weddings a half hour before our reserved registration time and, with great trepidation, started calling Kolya and Galya a few minutes later. A dozen calls later and exactly one minute before the ceremony was scheduled to begin our witnesses actually appeared. However, everything turned out well. We got our passports stamped and signed the registry. We then rode in the back of a rented Chaika (the big old black Soviet-built equivalent of a Mercedes that whisked important officials around the streets of Moscow) to all the traditional places newlyweds visited—Red Square, Lenin Hills, tomb of the unknown soldier, and so forth. That evening we had a table for eight reserved at the restaurant of the Hotel Berlin. Since Sergei Sergeevich was on duty and since all the waiters knew us, we got the best service available in all of Moscow. It was a memorable day, the culmination of nearly five years of joy and pain, anxiety, and anticipation.

The following day my visa was due to expire and, consequently, I was forced to leave the country of my new bride on the very next morning following my wedding. So we did a very Russian thing. We partied well into the early and mid-hours of the night, first in the restaurant, then in my suite at the hotel. Sufficiently into the night that it was already well into the morning when, startled at the lateness of the hour and reminded of my imminent departure, I began hastily to pack and make other preparations for leaving the hotel. This was to be only the first of numerous trips to Moscow that I made over the next several months at the end of which I was forced to depart Moscow alone until Tanya finally got all the permits and authorizations allowing her to accompany me.

JARVIS'S VISIT

In the summer of 1975, a couple of years before our marriage, I was invited to negotiations in Moscow for a complex line of equipment to clean and to process corn seeds. In order to handle the many technical questions that were bound to arise, I made arrangements to have several specialists join me from their places of work in the midwest. There were three of them under the directorship of a certain Mel Jarvis, who was also accompanied by his wife. They were to fly to Chicago, where they would make a connection to New York, where I planned to meet them. From there, we had a five-to-six hour flight to London, then a connection to Moscow for an additional four-hour flight. By the time they arrived in New York, they were already well lubricated. By the time we were halfway to London, they were completely inebriated. In a way, this was fortunate, since they then slept most of the way to Moscow.

Arrival and Passport Control

That was a particularly hot summer in Moscow. Furthermore, there were a large number of out-of-control fires in some of the peat bogs around the city. So it was not only stiflingly hot, there also was a terrible-smelling and somewhat toxic haze in the air all of which made the conditions in and around Moscow less than appealing. We arrived at Moscow airport at about 1:00 p.m. in these sultry conditions. Prior to the Olympics, which were to take place in Moscow in 1980—for which they were constructing a large and much more modern new airport—there was only one airport where international passengers could be processed. It was an incredibly obsolete facility: no air conditioning, one filthy toilet (with no toilet paper), no restaurants or other amenities, two or three ancient carousels for handling luggage, and hand processing of travel documents—no computers.

The first part of the agony began by walking into the terminal, a dirty, low-built gray building with sagging doors, translucent windows, and unsmiling, armed militia men at every turn. We entered the building and were greeted by—chaos. There were about ten to twelve wooden booths with narrow, gated walkways on one side where a small, grimy window was located with a slotted 4-inch opening under it for documents to be passed back and forth. Typically, there would be hundreds of people in the hall with only four to five booths manned (or womanned as the case might be, and frequently was). Lines sort of formed with knots of people in front of each booth.

The process was inordinately long term. As their turn would finally come, each individual would approach the window of the booth in front of him/her, slide documents through the slot, then wait. The person in the booth was always stony faced with beady eyes that stared at you unblinkingly for uncomfortably long periods of time. Frequently, the passport control personnel would compare your official photograph to your face a dozen times. Almost invariably there would come a moment when the immigration officer would press a button and wait for another uniformed individual to approach the booth. This was the most intimidating part of the entire process. The new individual would take your documents from the first person and walk off to some indeterminate destination. You would have all kinds of crazy notions going through your mind. Perhaps your photo resembled some notorious smuggler. Perhaps your name was similar to that of some arms dealer. Perhaps they thought you were an employee of the CIA. I'm sure now that it was all intended simply to intimidate the arrivals, especially Americans during the worst days of the cold war. But it worked. It really was intimidating! And certainly not intended to make the beginning of your stay in Moscow a pleasant experience. Eventually, the documents would be stamped and returned and you would be considered processed.

Retrieving Luggage

It took about an hour to get to the front of our line, then another forty minutes for me to get through and to shepherd my four charges through. Next part of the process was to retrieve luggage. Since only one carousel ever seemed to work at any given time and since international passengers' luggage was subject to special scrutiny, it always took a long time for suitcases to appear. This particular day was especially excruciating. Apparently, several other flights had arrived just before ours. Thus the baggage area was flooded with passengers looking for their things. Because of the heat, lack of air conditioning, and the large number of people in the hall, the air was stifling. Malodorous also because of the by now freely perspiring bodies and, of course, the burning peat moss.

Trying to make way through the milling passengers, we approached the only working carousel. At that moment, there was a piercing feminine scream. We did not immediately learn what had happened for the area was simply too crowded to determine anything. However, the screaming continued unabated for some substantial period of time. When I was finally able to make my way to the source of the noise—which was in the direction I was headed toward the carousel—I learned that a passenger had had a heart attack. He was lying on the floor and his wife was next to him screaming at the top of her lungs. Nobody seemed to be able to help, and, in fact, it transpired that the man was already dead. We later learned that the couple was French and had arrived about forty minutes before us on a flight from Paris. Ironically, it also turned out that the couple had entered a contest and won—the prize being an all-expenses paid week's vacation in Moscow. The poor man lay there with his wife alternately screaming and sobbing for about forty minutes before some airline worker had the decency to approach and cover him up with a blanket.

We waited for some lengthy period of time for our luggage; then it became apparent that it was not arriving on the same airplane as we had arrived. This was rather dismaying since it was not very easy in Moscow in those days to acquire simple items like soap and toothpaste to weather the period of waiting for suitcases to catch up. However, we proceeded to wade through customs—a fairly simple procedure for once since we had no baggage, thus nothing to declare—such as *Playboy* magazines, long playing records, jeans, cigarettes, or perfume all of which could fuel the black market. These particular items were very much in short supply and made great gifts because the recipient either wanted the items for himself or he could convert them into cash in a heartbeat.

Back in those days, there was a great shortage of hotels, even in Moscow and so you had to have a hotel assigned to you before being granted a visa. This process was normally ensured by issuing a hotel voucher to every arriving visitor at the same time as his/her visa was issued. The voucher advised the hotel the visitor should stay at and the dates of arrival and departure. The procedure was simple if time consuming. After enduring passport control, baggage retrieval, and customs, the arriving passenger had to seek out the Intourist desk (Intourist being the state bureaucracy for processing all international passengers whether in country for tourism or for business). There he would show his visa and voucher. The Intourist representative would check the voucher against a handwritten list (again, no computers). The process seemed interminable because you always had some sneaky fear that this would be the time they would not find your name—which meant that you had no hotel assigned to you. No hotel meant no place to stay—a very serious dilemma.

Moscow Hotels

There was a real class system in those days for Moscow hotels. First, there were non-Intourist establishments designated for the use of high-ranking party members and enterprise directors from around the Soviet Union. These were never an option for any foreigners except, possibly, high-ranking diplomats officially representing their country. Then there were the standard Intourist hotels where western foreigners stayed—especially visitors who carried business visas. These were the hotels considered more or less respectable for these "high-class" visitors. After that were third and fourth-tier hotels and hostels meant for common Soviet citizens and other less-important guests such as vacationers from East European countries or visitors from Africa or the Far East.

The Intourist hotels we were normally assigned to were such stalwarts as the appropriately named Intourist (the Soviet equivalent of a modern high rise), the Rossiya (a structure of monstrous proportions located between the Kremlin and the Moscow River), the National (an older building of rather seedy elegance), and the somewhat similar Metropole. We always requested rooms at the Hotel Berlin—another comparatively old edifice—and usually were given vouchers for our stay there. This trip, however, I was one of five people traveling together, and since there were not usually five rooms available at the Berlin at any given time, I anticipated that our delegation would be assigned other accommodations. We approached the Intourist desk, I with more than a little trepidation, concerned about where we would end up staying. I handed over our five vouchers and watched with increasing unease as the Intourist representative scanned the half-dozen or so pages of illegible handwriting without checking off a single one of our names. She was, however, very thorough: she checked through the entire list at least three times before announcing that she had found no matches. Our worst fears were realized; we were without hotel. The Intourist representative merely shrugged her shoulders and pronounced that there was nothing she could do, so we should just wait—a code word that meant we sit in the shabby airport all night. After pondering our predicament for a moment, I decided to call an old friend—Kolya—the very same one who was later to become witness at our wedding.

Kolya

Kolya was tall and thin. He had a prominent, beaked nose, very lively, blue eyes, and thin, sandy hair. He always seemed to be smiling with eyes dancing mischievously. I had first met Kolya some months before when he rescued my boss and me from an unpleasant situation. We had been to a very late business dinner. At the conclusion, everyone else dispersed and we were left standing on the street alone. Despite the size of Moscow, it was like a provincial town after midnight with streets nearly deserted, very few vehicles or pedestrians abroad. Sometimes it was simply impossible to find a taxi especially when it was raining like it was at this moment. However, there was one useful tradition in Moscow those days that could sometimes solve the problem of no taxis. It was perfectly acceptable (if slightly risky) to flag down any private vehicle passing by. The driver would almost always stop since people were constantly on the lookout to augment their meager salaries in some way or another. The driver would stop right in front of you, then wheel down the passenger-side window just far enough to communicate. First question, "Where to?" If he got an acceptable answer to that question, that is, you wanted to go somewhere that was more or less on his way so that it was not a severe inconvenience, he would ask the second, "How much?" You would know that your answer to the first question was not acceptable if the driver—without comment—simply closed the window and drove off. In response to "How much?" you would have to come up with a reasonable offer of cash, usually somewhat more than what you knew the normal fare to be, sometimes up to twice as much. A pack of western cigarettes would also go a long way in persuading the driver to pick you up.

On the night in question, Kolya happened to be driving by while we were standing forlornly in the dark street. He immediately stopped and agreed to take us to our destination for a pack of cigarettes. He didn't even want cash. A smoker myself back then, I always carried an extra pack or two of cigarettes with me for just such a situation. It turned out that Kolya was a very loquacious individual. From the moment, he picked us up until he dropped us off at our hotel he never stopped talking. In fact, his conversation was witty and humorous and very entertaining. When we parted company, he announced that he was actually a taxi driver by profession and that he would be pleased to ferry us around anywhere we wanted day or night. He scrawled his phone number on a piece of paper, handed it to me, and suggested that

I call any time. Over the next several months, I had occasion to call Kolya many times, and he always accommodated me by ferrying me around to wherever I needed to travel. We got to know each other rather well and formed a friendship that lasted many years afterward.

So when the Jarvis group and I were stranded in Moscow with no luggage and no place to go, I called Kolya. We were miserable—hot and sweaty, exhausted from the long trip, hungry, and extremely frustrated from the twin disasters of lost luggage and no hotel to go to for freshening up, having a bite to eat, and getting some rest. Also, I suspect that a couple members of our group were rather severely hung-over. Without hesitation, Kolya invited us to his apartment and apologized that he was not in a position to pick us up personally. I got his address, and we exited the terminal to hail a taxi. It required a small bribe in US dollars since there were five of us, and it was illegal for taxis to accommodate more than four people besides the driver. We squeezed in and were at Kolya's apartment building in half-an-hour.

Kolya and his wife, Galya, greeted us very warmly. Within an hour, we had freshened up and had a small supper. Galya and Kolya then retrieved from some place unbeknownst to the rest of us several mattresses, blankets, sheets, and pillows. This was a typical Soviet-style apartment—one bedroom, living cum dining room, small kitchen, and tiny bathroom. So all the bedding was put on the floor of the living room—which just about covered all the space available. Everyone was put down for the night, and Kolya and I repaired to the miniature balcony. It was still very warm outside, but at least the smell of the burning peat moss had somewhat abated. Kolya and I stayed out on the balcony until dawn, playing chess, smoking, and drinking scotch whiskey, and chatting about everything in general and nothing in particular.

AT THE OSTANKINO

Next morning I called an emergency number at the US Embassy. We were advised to go to the commercial office while relevant personnel at the embassy tried to locate accommodations for us. We gathered together our meager belongings, hired a taxi, and made our way to the designated site. Luckily, there were sofas and divans in a lounge area where the five of us could begin to recuperate somewhat. Later that day, we were informed that rooms had been found at a local hotel called Ostankino—definitely no more than two stars, but very acceptable to us in our condition. We headed out to the hotel, checked in, and bade each other a good rest until the next day when the real work would begin.

It was now Sunday, and I wanted desperately to see Tanya. Since it was still relatively early in the evening, I made contact and suggested that she come join me at the hotel. She arrived in good time, and we proceeded to catch each other up on our respective lives since we had last spent time together. Just after ten o'clock the telephone rang. It was the main clerk from reception advising us that "As we should have known, visitors are not allowed in guests' rooms after 10:00 p.m." We grabbed a half-full bottle of whiskey and left the hotel.

Outside was a very mild evening with only a lingering smell from the peat moss fires—very pleasant. We wandered around the hotel territory for a short while and found a pretty spot with bushes and flowering shrubs. There, next to the wall of the hotel, we continued to sip from the bottle and chat about what was transpiring in our lives.

Meeting Vitya

Presently, a policeman approached us and demanded to see our "documents." Tanya had no trouble in presenting her passport in short order, and I explained that mine was temporarily not available since I had just checked into the hotel and, as a foreigner, had had to surrender it. Tanya hastily added that I was from a technical organization in Poland that had been doing business with the Soviet Union for some time. Had it become known to him that I was actually an American and that I had arrived in Moscow on Saturday, but checked in only on Sunday, it would have gotten extremely complicated in very short order.

To begin with, Americans were very unpopular those years, so the authorities did everything possible to make our lives more difficult when visiting their city. There would have been very detailed questioning about why it took a full thirty hours from arrival time at the airport till check-in at the hotel. Very strict regulations were in force that required immediate check-in by all foreigners. And perhaps most serious of all would have been my connection with Kolya, a black marketeer and thief, and the fact that five foreigners stayed overnight at his flat. Foreigners were forbidden to spend any substantial periods of time in locals' living quarters, and this would have caused Kolya and Galya considerable misery.

The policeman believed Tanya immediately. After all, I was staying at a definite third-(if not fourth) rate hotel—where no self-respecting western businessman would stay, and my Russian was much better than theirs would have been. To solidify the connection and to dispel any lingering doubts, Tanya offered the policeman a drink of whiskey. He had little problem in accepting; the number of opportunities he would have to taste good quality western scotch would be miniscule. Our conversation became much more sociable and all further questions about documents or anything else official were dropped.

We continued standing around, taking turns at the bottle, the contents of which became increasingly depleted. Conversation became more animated and soon we were trading jokes and slapping each other on the back, having a good old time. Presently, our newfound friend—I believe his name was Vitya—suggested that we go swimming. He explained that he knew of a beautiful pond located not too far from where we were partying and, since it was such a mild evening, it would be quite enjoyable to take a dip. How would we get there, we wondered? No problem said he, and showed us his motorcycle.

Midnight Dip

Somehow the policeman managed to get astride the vehicle, and Tanya and I scrambled aboard. We clung to the back of the machine as the policeman gunned it furiously and tore out of the parking lot, pebbles clattering while creating a rooster tail behind us. We drove off through the night, Tanya and I desperately hanging on to the bike and to each other. We were quite impressed with Vitya's driving for he was steering with one hand only as he gaily waved the bottle of Johnny Walker with the other, and keeping to a more or less straight path despite the not inconsiderable amount that he had imbibed. Presently, we came to a pond where our host—as we now acknowledged—parked the motorcycle and immediately celebrated our arrival with a toast and a sustained pull from the bottle.

Vitya made it clear that Tanya and I should not hesitate to plunge in. He declined to wade in himself, however, explaining that, first, he couldn't swim and, second, he felt that he should be "on the look-out," after all, as a militia man on shift he was on duty. Tanya and I did shed some clothes, jump in, and splash about for some time. I must admit that it was very refreshing after the very warm evening and the several toasts that we had washed down with the Johnny Walker. After ten or fifteen minutes of this enjoyable activity I heard a rueful "Oops!" from Tanya. Turned out that she had not taken her glasses off, and they finally slipped down the end of her by now slippery nose and were swallowed up by the murky water. We spent a few minutes in fruitless search, but quickly realized that it was a fool's errand to look for those spectacles in five feet of midnight dark pond water.

By now, our host and driver had dozed off. Eventually, Tanya and I realized that we had better be on our way. With difficulty, we roused Vitya and advised him that we needed to go home; the next day was a very important workday for both of us, and it was already quite late. However, Vitya was rather unresponsive: his head lolled to the side and his eyes fluttered open a time or two, and then stayed shut. We gave up on him and went off to seek a taxi. We arrived at Tanya's place around 1:00 in the morning and were so exhausted that we promptly fell asleep. At about 4:00 in the morning, I awoke with horror to realize that I was a far distance from the hotel and was going to have a devilish time meeting Jarvis and his colleagues at 6:00 a.m. as we had agreed the day before.

Back to Reality

Seriously concerned, I fled the apartment with Tanya right behind. She felt that she could greatly enhance my chances of finding a taxi at that unlikely hour. In fact, she was eventually able to flag down the driver of a private auto who agreed to take me to the hotel for a handsome sum of money and a pack of American cigarettes. She decided to accompany me as the driver was a bit seedy looking, and she was worried about me being a foreigner and him possibly taking advantage of me in some way. However, we flew across town without incident and got to my hotel about the time I was slated to meet my group. I exited the cab and rushed off to the hotel. On the way, I had to pass the cafeteria where, much to my dismay, all members of the Jarvis group were standing in line to receive breakfast. I sheepishly explained that I had been out and got detained and that I would join them in a matter of minutes. They good-naturedly accepted this, and I rushed off to freshen myself up, change into different clothes, and join them. Later, I discovered that on the way back to her apartment, Tanya was in a rather serious car accident and, though not hurt too badly, had considerable skin stripped off her legs due to the collision she and her driver had suffered.

I quickly got myself into more respectable shape and rushed off to join the Jarvis group, after which we had some breakfast and went off to our first official meeting. The remainder of their stay in Moscow was relatively free of adventure in comparison to what had occurred up to now. We had very intensive technical and commercial negotiations every day with the buyers and representatives from the Ministry of Foreign Trade. And every evening we would go over the day's discussions and formulate strategy for the following day. At one point, we were quite optimistic that we would be awarded the contract which would have been in the region of $6.5 million. Alas, at the last moment another foreign company undercut us by such a substantial margin that we could no longer compete. Many years later, I learned that the other supplier installed such inferior equipment with equally poor technology that the plant never worked properly and that the money spent was considered a total waste.

KALININ

Not too long after I started working for the company, I was asked to accompany a group of British businessmen on a one-day trip to a small town called Kalinin, which was situated north of Moscow on the route to Leningrad (now St. Petersburg). Joining that group was a colleague of mine—Brendan—from the center of the British textile equipment-manufacturing sector. There were some seven or eight of them, technical specialists, and we were going to Kalinin to see about the feasibility of renovating an aged wool-spinning mill. The reason for the group being from Britain was that they represented several British manufacturers that would actually supply the equipment and technology if we were fortunate in getting the contract.

I had arranged to meet them at their hotel at a fairly early hour with a bus for transporting the entire group. It was immediately clear that the British group was very much the worse for wear. The explanation was simple. Late the previous evening they had returned from a rapid-fire trip to the south—I believe Rostov-on-Don—where they had been run ragged for forty-eight hours. The combination of marathon sessions of technical conversations with equally marathon sessions of eating and drinking had certainly taken their toll. Every one of them was suffering from the multiple effects of varying time zones, exhausting travel, complicated technical discussions, and excessive food and alcohol. Add to this the fact that they had gotten precious little sleep the night before we were due to depart for Kalinin.

Technical Matters

Kalinin was about two hours away from Moscow so, in a sense, it was a blessing for it gave them a much-needed opportunity to snooze a little in advance of another round of frenetic activity. After jolting over bad roads for the next couple hours, we arrived at the factory around nine o'clock in the morning, were greeted by half-a-dozen executives from the company and invited into a conference room for a get-acquainted session. We were offered soft drinks, tea, and cookies for a little snack and spent the rest of the first hour setting an agenda. There was unanimous agreement on a schedule that included a tour of the factory, some initial technical discussions, a light lunch and further, more detailed, technical questions and answers until the end of the day—at which time we assumed we would pack ourselves back into the bus and head home to Moscow. There was a sense of jubilation among the British specialists for the schedule appeared to preclude any serious eating and drinking sessions.

The rest of the day was fairly straightforward. Following a leisurely walk through the factory including many stops for clarification of questions regarding equipment, we returned to the conference room. Both sides made introductory remarks and then we broke for a light lunch. Afterward the two sides entered into a lengthy and detailed technical discussion that lasted until nearly six o'clock in the evening. At that point, the factory director announced that we had finished for the day and that we had accomplished everything she had planned for. The British visitors breathed an almost audible sigh of relief; they thought they would soon be on their way back to their hotel for a much-needed rest.

Dinner Near Kalinin

When we got on the bus and set off, however, we realized almost immediately that we were heading in a completely different direction. Sure enough, after a twenty-five-minute ride we pulled up to a rustic wooden inn somewhere in the forest near Kalinin. We exited the bus and were ushered into the facility where we saw a large table set for twenty people and laid out with enough provisions for fifty or more—including at least one full bottle of vodka for each place setting. Then began a round of toasts and snacks that lasted for the next six hours. The poor Brits—who were already in considerable pain from their excursion to Rostov—quickly became rather inebriated. But they were very game; they tried manfully to match their hosts drink for drink. When our hosts mercifully decided to call it a night a little after midnight, we piled everyone back into the bus and left for Moscow. However, the night was not yet completely over, for the director thoughtfully sent two of her deputies to accompany us on the return trip—with a couple bottles of good Armenian brandy.

Some hour or hour and a half later the moans that had been barely audible to that point became much more frantic. The enormous quantity of liquid that almost everyone had consumed was leading to some serious bladder distension. After a brief conference between the two factory deputy directors and the bus driver, we pulled over to the side of the road where the men (there were no women aboard) tumbled out and lined up near the bus overlooking an embankment. Since it was rather late and there was no traffic, they felt that it was safe to stand at the edge of the road and urinate into the void over the shoulder of the road. And so taking turns, three or four at a time, the foreign visitors as well as their hosts were occupied for the next ten minutes. At some moment during this activity, I noticed one tattered hand emerge from the blackness of the embankment. This was followed by another hand, then the equally bedraggled and soiled head and shoulders of my colleague, Brendan, who was pleading with the others to cease their sprinkling activity—at least until he was again secure on the road. He finally crawled up out of the pit with spectacles hanging from his left ear, a large crack running the full length of the other lens, which was drooping down near his mouth. I don't think he found the situation humorous, but the others all howled with laughter and wondered aloud if he had got sprayed very badly.

I never did find out how or even when Brendan fell into the abyss, but I was always glad that he appeared when he did, for just a few minutes later we resumed our return to Moscow. We would most likely not have realized that he was missing until arriving back at the hotel, and then it would have been almost impossible to find him on that dark desolate road. For months afterward, I was regularly reminded of the episode for Brendan made several trips to Moscow while I was there, and his failure to repair his glasses in a timely fashion made the crack in his lens appear ever more prominent.

RUSSIAN TRAINS

Since Kalinin was located a relatively short distance from Moscow, it was deemed desirable and convenient to travel there by bus. For longer distances, however, Russians (and—depending upon circumstances—foreigners) had the choice of trains or planes to get to their destination. Soviet citizens had a cultural preference for traveling by train rather than plane when feasible (not, for example, when going from Moscow to Vladivostok which could take over a week). A typical trip starts in the late afternoon or evening and arrives at destination the following morning. Locals party with food and plenty of drink—usually vodka, then go to sleep until near the time of arrival the next morning. At which time, they freshen up and go about their business. The overnight trip for most passengers was simply a change in venue for sleeping before the next day's work and an occasion for a miniparty. Unfortunately, it was never a pleasurable experience for me. Because of the poor design of the rail cars and tracks, the execrable maintenance of the equipment and the arbitrariness of scheduling bureaucrats, trains tended to clack along at maximum speeds of 30-40 miles an hour with frequent stops. Each time the train starts up again, it is as if the operator is responding to a challenge of how many passengers he can roll off their cots onto the floor. The trains jerk unmercifully and make such an excessive racket that I was never truly able to sleep.

In Soviet times, there were basically three classes of travel on medium distance or overnight train routes. There was the so-called general or "hard" category—long wagons with wooden benches arranged along one side in a direction perpendicular to that in which the train would travel. There was an aisle lengthwise on the other side to allow access to the seats themselves or the toilets located at either end of each wagon or the space between cars where the men would usually gather to smoke, tell tales, and quaff a bit of vodka. These wagons were not adorned with any amenities whatsoever. There were no partitions, nor doors; therefore, there was no privacy. In the winter people, would board with damp fur coats; in the summer, there were countless sweaty, unwashed bodies. These factors combined with the paucity of toilets resulted in a distinctly objectionable stench that made all passengers from other compartments avoid the "general" wagons religiously. There was a tier of benches over the ones on the floor in order to accommodate more passengers on top. All passengers slept on the benches without the benefit of mattresses or blankets. There was no air conditioning in the summer and heating in the colder months was minimal at best. Trips for these poor people were the trips from hell. But they were inexpensive, costing only a few pennies in local currency.

Next step up was the "coupe," a partitioned wagon with compartments holding four passengers each. The configuration was two benches across the length of the car with two more situated on top as bunks. Four people could be accommodated, and unless they were traveling together, did not know who would be their compartment mates until they actually arrived and entered the car. This was a standard coupe. Then there were so-called "soft" coupes with a little more padding on the seats, slightly nicer linen to sleep in, and a tiny tablecloth over the miniscule table. There were also four glasses provided for passengers' tea.

The third category was a luxury accommodation called "SV" or special wagon (the Russian version of wagon beginning with the letter v). This was a compartment partitioned off from the rest of the car thus allowing for some privacy. There were seats for two and a little table. At night, the seats were converted into beds with semisoft mattresses, sheets, blankets, and pillows. There was also a neat little tablecloth and glasses for tea with usually a couple pieces of candy to complete the luxury. Each compartment was equipped with a door that could be locked from the inside. Of course, each higher category of accommodation carried a concomitantly higher price tag.

ZHLOBIN

A couple years after my inaugural trip to the Soviet Union, we negotiated one of the largest contracts in the company's history—all the equipment to furnish what would be the largest artificial fur factory in the world. The Soviets had been actively selling their natural furs in the international market place for many years. The fur itself was such an important source for much needed hard currency and of such good quality and competitive price that there was a persistent shortage of the product for the Soviet populace itself. So somewhere in the upper reaches of the hierarchy the decision was handed down that since there was no home-grown technology, a factory to produce artificial fur as well as the manufacturing expertise would be purchased from abroad. The particular consortium of suppliers we represented won the contract, and we were responsible for fabricating and shipping the equipment on time, installing it at the site, and ensuring that it worked within the parameters guaranteed by the producers.

The factory was to be located in a small town called Zhlobin, located in the Belorussian Republic, not far to the north of a direct western route from Moscow to Poland. My first trip to Zhlobin was in the winter. A representative from the FTO accompanied me as was fairly standard practice. We boarded a train in the early evening and shivered through the next couple hours until it was time to take to our berths. The standard, non-luxury compartment—our accommodations for the night—held four narrow bunk beds. During the hours when passengers were up and about, the top bunks were typically folded up against the walls in order not to hinder the movements of the four individuals. There was a tiny foldout table situated in the center of the two stationary bottom bunks in the aisle opposite the entryway, right up against the window. With the table in the horizontal position, there was just barely room for the compartment's four passengers.

Unless four people were traveling together, passengers were simply thrown together helter-skelter. So it was the luck of the draw that determined your cabin mates on any given journey. They could be all women, all men, or they could be any combination in between. On this particular occasion, all four travelers ended up being of the male variety. When the FTO representative and I arrived at our designated location onboard, our two fellow passengers were already in attendance. Since they were both seated on one side, we determined that we should take the other. My escort asked whether I had any preference over top or bottom. When I answered in the negative, he politely offered to take the top. Only problem was I couldn't retire until he decided that it was time to put his cot down, make it up with the bedding provided and climb in for the night.

Before the train even began rolling out of the station, our two compartment mates started to lay their provisions out onto the little table. Before my astonished eyes, there appeared a chicken, several hard boiled eggs, tomatoes, pieces of garlic, greens such as scallions, dill and cilantro, salami, pepperoni, and a kind of bologna. They placed two bottles of beer on the table and then added a bottle of vodka. My travel partner was unfazed, but I did not expect this; it was my first real train trip in the Soviet Union. I learned then, and it was confirmed many times since that a train ride was occasion for feasting on a fairly grand scale. The two gentlemen started in with a shot of vodka, a swill of beer, and several mouthfuls of food. Soon they were asking us to join them. I'm not sure whether they simply felt sorry that we had nothing with us or just felt embarrassed that they were eating while others were not, but they soon became fairly insistent that we also partake of the bounty laid out before us. It is even more likely that it was simple Russian hospitality and generosity, which were usually in bountiful supply. In later years, I became completely convinced that this was the case for the invitation to compartment mates to partake of one's repast on a train, and this was a common occurrence even though the travelers were usually total strangers.

We had no choice but to accommodate them, and so began a three-hour session of belting back shots of vodka (turned out they had not one but several bottles) followed by snacking off the ample stock of food they had in their various bags and satchels. In a short period of time, we all became fast friends. We seemed to forget that it was probably no more than fifty degrees in the cabin. After a while, I wanted nothing more than to wrap myself up in the meager blankets afforded to each of us, but the others seemed content to sit there, eat, drink, and gossip. Our cabin mates were intrigued over the fact that fate had deposited an American in their midst and asked me a multitude of questions—more out of curiosity than hostility. So it was rather late by the time they decided to pack it in for the night, remove the detritus from the table, and assume positions in their respective berths. They appeared to have no trouble falling asleep; indeed, after only a few minutes, there was a veritable concert of wheezes, snores, and whistles. It became clear to me while I tried vainly to fall asleep that Russians had great experience sleeping wherever and whenever they could grab a snooze. I, on the other hand, tossed and turned for hours, trying to find some comfortable position that would allow a modicum of rest. However, the various noises and sounds emitted from my three fellow passengers plus the racket of the train itself hounded me regardless of the position I selected.

After what seemed an interminable period of time spent clattering and clacking along at probably no more than thirty miles an hour, stopping at a dozen way-stations, then jerking into start-up mode again, we finally began to approach the station Gomel. Because of the continual stops and start-ups and the accompanying rattling of the wheels, I had gotten virtually no sleep at all—despite the fairly prodigious amount of alcohol I had ingested. I was advised to go to the rest room and freshen up, for we were to get off the train at Gomel. Which was not yet our final destination.

Arrival at Factory

At Gomel, we were met by a man who turned out to be our driver for the rest of the trip. He bustled us into a jeep-like vehicle, and we began bumping our way over the worst road I have ever been on. Full of ruts and potholes, the road was paved only in some sections. Elsewhere, there was nothing but snow-covered roadways carved out of the forests and the swamps. We jounced and bounced our way over a wasteland of humps and hills, bends and curves for a full three hours. In time, we arrived at Zhlobin, a rather unprepossessing complex of low buildings and mostly unpaved streets. Its only claim to fame was the future fake fur plant we were going to equip. I was put up at the local hotel in a room that measured about six feet by eight feet. Next day, I was charged seven rubles for the pleasure. Back in those days that was worth about ten dollars.

I was taken to the factory and given a tour. My hosts showed me where the equipment was to be placed, and we spent some time on the timing of shipments, sending technicians to the plant, installation of machinery, and actual start up. There were hundreds of questions and requests for additional information all of which I dutifully noted down. We finished late in the afternoon and then were whisked back to Gomel by the same jeep-like vehicle that brought us there the day before. The train ride back to Moscow was pretty much a carbon copy of the trip the day before with no additional adventures and no more sleep.

Next time, I went to Zhlobin was another six months later. By then, our equipment had arrived and been placed in the factory for installation. In addition, by then, our hosts had completed construction of a small apartment building dedicated to our technical support team that would be in residence for six to nine months while the equipment was being installed and fine-tuned. Our people had been there for a couple weeks, and it was my job to make sure that everything was going according to schedule and to determine whether any problems were in the offing so as to resolve them ahead of time. I arrived pretty much the same way as before, but since our schedule called for us to visit the plant that same day, we drove directly there for a strategy session. Toward the end of our discussions, one of our hosts broke free and dialed a number into the local phone. The Soviet telephone system was notoriously inefficient, so I was not at all surprised at the deafening shouts that ensued when his connection was complete. However, the words he was bellowing into the phone at the top of his lungs were something I always remembered with real amusement: "Turn the heat and water on in the American hotel!" It transpired that in a typically Soviet effort at conservation, the centrally controlled heat and water were shut off every morning as our technicians left for the factory and turned on again at the end of the day to mark their return. But since the individual at the heat and water controls did not know when the technicians would finish their work for the day, someone from the factory had to phone this information in each time. We were driven to the new apartment complex—a luxury compared to the local hotel I stayed at first trip. I also found amusing their designation for our temporary residence in their town as "the American hotel."

The Fishing Trip

Next morning we all went to the factory where we were busy all day resolving some of the many issues that inevitably come up when you are installing twenty-five million dollars' worth of machinery. I had been forewarned that at the end of the workday we would be "going fishing." I did not question this. At about four o'clock, we finished our discussions, left the technical staff at the plant and set off. We drove to a pier where four of us got into a very powerful looking boat. I had put on a sweater under my jacket and was very pleased at the foresight, for it was quite cool in the open boat. We motored up river—the famous Dnieper—for forty minutes or so and then turned in toward shore where we tied up to a dock. A couple of men were standing by the riverbank with fish poles. It turned out that these men were part of our group for the evening. We were eventually joined by another half dozen men (yes, this was a chauvinistic crowd) to bring the total size of our party to eleven or twelve.

We climbed up a rather steep set of stairs at the top of which was located a wooden cabin. Outside a fire had been started, and here another two men bustled about gathering firewood, breaking it up into pieces, and feeding the flames. Presently, the fishermen appeared from below, each with a bucket carrying their catch. At this stage, the men fashioned a trivet over the fire and suspended a pail half-full of water from its top. Next thing I knew one of them tossed a whole chicken sans feathers into the water. A short time later scaled, but still whole, fish were dropped in, then were added potatoes, carrots, and onions. By now, they had rigged things up so that the trivet could accommodate two pails. We were all invited into the cabin and seated at a long table. I was quite surprised at there being but one bottle of vodka on the table. I had attended enough social events in the Soviet Union to know that this crew could handle at least ten or more bottles. My surprise turned out to be short-lived. As soon as one bottle was emptied, another was placed on the table to replace it. I never did figure out where they were coming from, but there seemed to be an endless supply. We were each given a large deep dish and soon the soup was ladled with generous pieces of fish, chicken, and vegetables. And thus did we spend the next six hours or so—eating the soup, listening to toasts, and knocking back copious quantities of vodka. Sometime during this feast, a couple of the men retrieved guitars from somewhere and started up a songfest. When I later asked what they had meant by "going fishing," they explained that that was precisely what we had been engaged in for the past seven to eight hours. Regardless, it was an unforgettable and most pleasant evening, and my first experience with *ukha* or fish soup.

Because of the size and complexity of the artificial fur factory we were equipping it required several trips to Zhlobin over the next few years to help in the resolution of various problems. So it was that I became used to train travel, which turned out to be good preparation for the dozens of other train trips I made in the future to a fascinating array of cities and towns around the country. In the early days of my travel to the Soviet Union, travel to any place outside Moscow was very strictly regulated.

The foreigner had to have an invitation from a certified and authorized organization having an official connection to that city. All travel arrangements were made for the foreigner—usually by a representative of the FTO he was working with, and then the foreigner was accompanied on his journey by another representative of that same FTO. This way a full accounting of all the visitor's movements could be made to the appropriate personnel at the FTO back in Moscow. From there, the report would make its way up the chain of bureaucrats until it reached the magical place where such documents were collected and stored. Over the years, however, regulations loosened considerably, and the foreign visitor was allowed to travel to outside areas somewhat more freely.

Buzuluk

Shortly after this became possible, I began to have a number of conversations with potential partners in the garment industry. Most of these entities were located away from Moscow, to the east of the capital. An acquaintance of mine in the United States was an importer of men's apparel and constantly on the lookout for new, preferably inexpensive, suppliers. From my old days in the textile raw materials business, I had many contacts in the downstream phases of the industry, and these readily advised me where I could go for leads in the apparel business. One such recommendation was a trade organization in Orenburg with links to suppliers throughout the area. Now, Orenburg was a fairly large city in the easternmost section of the European part of the Russian Federation just west of the Ural Mountains. It was a very important industrial and scientific center, and the administrative capital of an area rich in oil and gas production, extraction of a wide variety of minerals and manufacturing.

We were able to catch a local flight to Orenburg, where we stayed overnight at a typical seedy, run-down hotel. The lack of normal amenities did not particularly bother us, however, since our goal was farther on, not Orenburg itself. After a hasty breakfast of cold wieners, hard-boiled eggs, black bread, and tepid tea, we left early next day by car for Buzuluk. This was reported to me as housing a very large cut-and-sew operation that turned out a wide assortment of garments. The name of the town alone did not augur well; it had an unpleasant ring to it that made me a bit apprehensive. In any event, it did not take us long to exit the Orenburg city limits; from then on, there was nothing but wasteland. Gas and oil wells began to appear on both sides of the road with ever-increasing frequency, and other than the wells, there was nothing: not a tree or a shrub, not even a small hillock—just rocks and sand and the interminable wells. By now, the smell from the pumping gas and oil permeated everything so that even with the windows shut tight the odor was suffocating. No sign of life at all—until we came upon a large tractor-trailer that had jackknifed across half the road's single lane and what passed for the shoulder. We could barely scrape past, but we did manage to overtake without even the pretense of halting. When I asked why we didn't stop to see if the victims needed help, the answer was "They know how to take care of themselves." Not a whit concerned about the condition of the crash victims our hosts assured us it was only another two hours to our destination.

Sure enough in another two hours or thereabouts, we approached a haze-covered gray city that appeared to slump under a burden of unrelieved drudgery and tedium. The fact that there was considerable cloud cover did not help the overall feeling of bleak depression. It was as if all hope in life had dissipated, all aspirations come to naught. There were factories—relatively small ones to be sure—but smoke-spewing structures that provided a setting for the grinding slog of an existence that apparently varied not at all from one day to the next. Interspersed between the factories were rows and rows of three- to six-story edifices that housed the poor victims of Buzuluk's factory class. The buildings were an exact match of the plants—a dismal gray—and were situated in great clusters of identical cement monstrosities. I was always amazed how anyone could ever find his way home, for each complex was exactly the same, each building was the same, and each entryway was the same. Without actually visiting them, you knew that the apartments themselves were also duplicates of one another. The entire picture left one with an indescribable feeling of misery and hopelessness. From the moment we arrived at the town, I counted the minutes until we would leave.

After a little maneuvering, we arrived at a hotel—quite possibly the only one in Buzuluk. We registered, and I was given a key and directed to my room. I went up to bathe after the trip, change clothes, and prepare for dinner. My first negative impression of the place came almost immediately; when I lifted the toilet lid, I saw a bowl full of brown water—not just a little dirty or rusty—dark brown as if directly from a mud puddle. I used the facility and, upon flushing, noted that the replacement water was just as brown as what it replaced. With a certain amount of dread, I approached the sink. Turning on the faucet, I was horrified to note that only this same brown liquid was available for washing up as well. There was no bathtub or shower, so I did not have these facilities to worry about. There was a pitcher of water on the shelf—presumably for drinking, but I resolved not to let this water even near my lips. I was able though to use this liquid to clean up a little. I changed and went downstairs. I did not complain for this was a situation the locals were accustomed to and found acceptable, and I wanted to avoid sounding like a spoiled complainer.

We went out to a local restaurant for dinner hosted by the factory personnel who had invited us. It was a typical Russian dinner with lots of greasy food and copious amounts of alcohol. Toasts were frequent and the food was plentiful, and after the long trip, I soon found myself wishing for a comfortable hotel room with a snug and restful environment to relax in. Thankfully, the real evening's celebration being scheduled for the morrow, we broke for the night and returned to the hotel.

Night at the Hotel

I washed up with the remainder of the water in the pitcher and made myself ready for bed. That particular piece of furniture was an iron-framed, single-sized unit with thin mattress and a covering of grayish-white sheet and thin, spotted blanket (I did not want to think what might have caused the stains). The bed was situated snug up against the wall, parallel to it, so that one side would always be facing the room, the other the wall. When I was ready for bed, I turned out the lights at the last moment, slipped in on top of the threadbare mattress, and enveloped myself as much as possible in the sheet and blanket and tried to sleep. However, sleep was elusive to say the least, and only with considerable luck was I able to doze a little from time to time.

After a couple hours of this futile exercise, I suddenly went on full alert. First very faintly, then in an ever more pronounced way, there made itself audible to me a scuttling sound that traveled from one point on the wall next to me to another, much closer one. It soon became clear to me that an animal of some description (bigger than a cockroach but smaller than a mouse) was making its way along the vertical surface roughly in my direction. Whatever it was had tiny little feet with protruding nails that made a slight rattling sound as it moved along its way. Occasionally, it would pause for a second or two and then continue on its way. The pauses were as unnerving as the creature's movement, for I couldn't help but wonder if it was checking me out with some nefarious purpose in mind. Eventually, however, the thing hopped on my shoulder, ran down the length of my body and exited off onto the floor somewhere around my ankles. I must have broken some time record for quitting the bed, flinging off the scant coverings and hitting the light switch. I assessed the situation but could discern no living organisms of any kind or size. I was both relieved and concerned; relieved that there did not appear to be any more live things interested in competing with me over space, concerned that I never got to know what sort of living creature it was that had so brazenly came off the wall, visited me briefly then scuttled off to its own mysterious lair.

I took what few steps were possible. I pulled the bed away from the wall toward the center of the room where things crawling around or running up and down the vertical surfaces would have to travel a certain amount of floor space to get to my distressed self. I thoroughly checked the sheet, blanket, and pillow to ensure that there were no creatures already there. To make sure, I thoroughly and vigorously shook each of the bed coverings separately. I wrapped myself in the sheet and blanket and huddled there for the remainder of the night, not knowing whether or not to expect another unwelcome visitation. Needless to say, I did not get any sleep or rest.

In the morning, I washed up with water from the pitcher, which I had requested they refill, prepared the few things I had brought with me and got ready to be picked up for a day's work at the designated factory. It was a fairly intense work day with us squeezing as much effort into the time allotted as possible. Both my hosts from Orenburg and I wished to finalize all business issues so as to leave by the end of the day for our return trip. This would also allow us to beg off on the dinner our hosts had planned for at the close of the working session. We were successful, and much to our collective satisfaction and happiness departed for Orenburg in time to make it back before midnight. And so went my trip to Buzuluk the name of which will always be synonymous with creepy things scuttling up and down hotel room walls and brown water to bathe in.

VOLOGDA

Tanya and I were overdue for a trip back to the States; we hadn't been home in almost a year. But just before departure, I had to travel to the city of Vologda for one day's meetings with the local transit authorities in connection with the project I was working on. Since we knew ahead of time that it would be a rather long day, we made arrangements to stay overnight at an available hotel. We left on a Wednesday and were to return on Thursday. I had no concerns about any complications since we were not leaving for the United States until Saturday. There were three of us going, including my colleague Karl who possessed a car, and so we decided to drive as opposed to taking the train. We left very early on Wednesday so as to get there in time to complete all the work we had scheduled for ourselves. The trip there was uneventful; we arrived midmorning and went straight to the office of our local counterparts where we spent the rest of the day with the director and his deputy. We completed all our discussions and resolved all outstanding issues and were able to register at the hotel by early evening. I turned in my passport as was the requirement at all hotels in Russia.

Leaving for Moscow

We retired early, planning on a timely departure for the six-seven-hour return journey. When we prepared to leave, there was no one in attendance, so we simply dropped our keys on the reception counter and left. We had covered over two-thirds of our trip when we came upon a small town with narrow streets just teeming with traffic. Unfortunately, the truck driver behind us was not as careful as he needed to be and, without warning, struck us from behind rather forcibly. No one was hurt, but there was fairly serious damage to the rear of the car we were traveling in. Traffic accidents in Russia required very detailed reporting in order to assess damage and determine blame. It took us about four hours to sort out the bureaucratic red tape (and pay a few bribes—which definitely paved the way for a smoother resolution of the problem). At some time during this ordeal, I recalled that my briefcase was in the newly damaged trunk. With great dread, I began to recall the morning's events including the tossing of keys onto the reception counter and leaving the hotel *without* getting my passport back. I asked Karl to open the trunk so I could check my briefcase and verify the situation, for that's where I would have put the passport if I had received it back. He couldn't open the damaged trunk, of course, but as soon as I told him the reason for my panic, he also remembered that he had not gotten his passport back. Now it was no longer guesswork; we were without the very documents that validated our existence.

We rushed back to Moscow where we hoped to come up with some plan to retrieve our passports. Since Karl and I both planned to leave the country on Saturday, we were equally motivated. We started working the phones like mad, one calling our local colleagues in Vologda, the other trying to contact the hotel. We got through to the hotel almost immediately, only to be informed that, yes, they had noticed we had forgotten our passports, so they decided to hand them over to our colleague, Sasha, who promised to give them to us as soon as possible. Sasha worked with our counterparts in the town, but had to travel to Moscow the following day and had decided to stay at the hotel for convenience and catch an early train in the morning. I asked for his room number and started calling nonstop. There was no answer. Meantime, my colleague kept calling the office. The problem was that so much time had been consumed trying to sort out the accident that we were now calling after regular office hours.

After a couple hours of dialing in vain, Karl finally got through to a caretaker. He spent several minutes explaining why it was so important to locate the director or his deputy, or at least to determine their home telephone numbers. At about this same time, I finally got an answer at the hotel room in which I had previously been told Sasha was staying. The sounds he made were more incoherent mumbling and muttering than distinct words or phrases. It did not take me long to realize that whatever individual had picked up the receiver was so inebriated that he did not even know who was calling or even who *he* was. I called the receptionist again to confirm that I was, in fact, dialing the right number and that Sasha was actually registered in that room. To my horror, she confirmed both. Now we knew that our passports were in the possession of a person who could not utter a coherent word let alone remember where he had put our passports. And, in any event, he certainly would not be in any shape next morning to make the train to Moscow. I did try to make contact again to see if there was any possibility of making myself understood. For the next hour, however, I either got no response at all to my telephoning or the slurring at the other end was so disorienting that it was almost better not to get any response at all.

Karl was by now so exasperated over our lack of success that he suggested we get back in the car and return to Vologda. We discussed the idea and felt that we could travel there, retrieve our passports and still make it back by Friday evening—a full twelve hours before our departure to the States Saturday morning. It would be chancy but, we thought, doable. What gave us pause was the question of whether we would find Sasha and, if we did, whether we could even locate our passports. While we were mulling over the pros and cons of returning to Vologda, the phone rang with the first bit of good news we had since leaving Moscow. The caretaker called to pass on to us the director's home telephone number. This seemed to give us other options, so we started calling instead of jumping in the car again.

Voila! We got through first try! The woman of the house, the director's wife, advised us that her husband was not expected home right after work. He had to attend some meetings after which he planned to join a friend either at his house or at a local restaurant. She gave us the friend's phone number and the name of the restaurant they would most likely go to if that was their decision. We were able to elicit the number of the latter and immediately called both the restaurant and the friend's house, leaving frantic messages and calls for help at both. Then we sat back to wait. Waiting, however, is a genuinely negative experience when you're running out of options. We realized that if we continued to wait we would forfeit the possibility of going back to fetch the passports ourselves.

Rather than wait we started calling all three numbers again—the director's wife, his friend, and the restaurant, and leaving the same message over and over. At long last, our persistence was rewarded. The phone rang between our calls, and it was the director himself. When we explained the problem, he graciously offered to go to the hotel and try to meet with Sasha in person. More grateful than we could put into words we leaped at this possible solution. Again, we started to wait with great agitation, but this time with a much higher degree of optimism. Sure enough, in another hour or so, the phone rang again. The director informed us that not only had he found Sasha (who was still totally incoherent from alcohol intake); he located our passports and retrieved them. He even went so far as to charge a colleague with taking the next morning's train to Moscow and personally delivering our documents to us. It's nice when convoluted stories like this one have a happy ending. This one did indeed, for on the next day late in the afternoon our passports were in fact delivered to us—giving us a whole twelve hours of extra time before leaving the country.

EREVAN/ONWARD

There came a time when I had to go to Erevan, the capitol of Armenia. My assistant at the time, Maia, was a woman of about my own age, highly educated and extremely well connected in many of the ex-Soviet Republics. She and I took off on our flight to Erevan about three hours later than scheduled—fairly standard for those chaotic days shortly before the break-up of the Soviet Union, a time when practically no one was keeping house—especially in the airports. By the time, we arrived at the Armenian airport it was already about midnight. We left the airport complex and after driving through impenetrable darkness in a totally unfamiliar setting, ended up at someone's home well after 1:00 in the morning (I always figured a friend of a friend of a friend type situation, but never knew for sure). Which was a stroke of incredible luck, since to get into a hotel at that time of night would have been unimaginably difficult, probably even impossible. What wonderful people our hosts turned out to be! The lady of the house made us up a full and very delicious meal and gave us space to rest for the night. Total strangers and such wonderful hospitality. This was the warm hospitality for which Armenians are justifiably famous.

The next day we had a series of meetings that pretty much carried us through to the evening. Since it was still relatively early, we had little trouble in getting hotel rooms. When we finished in Erevan, we were scheduled to go to Tbilisi, the capitol of Georgia. There were serious problems with the commercial airlines at that time, so my assistant made arrangements with our soon-to-be hosts in Georgia to have us flown to Tbilisi in a private helicopter. The morning we were supposed to leave, we packed up and left for the airport. At the terminal, we met the two men who had been designated to assist us. They indicated that we should follow them.

The Helicopter

We began trundling our suitcases in their wake, across the tarmac. We walked and walked, and there appeared to be nothing in front of us but endless, cracked and crumbling asphalt. However, in time, we were able to make out—in the far distance—a helicopter. The closer we got the more acute became my feelings of dismay. The machine was unpainted, scratched, dirty, and dented. I have no idea what its age was, but it certainly went into the several decades category. One man opened the door, which stuck at first, then swung slowly outward with a mournful creak like the lid of a coffin in an old horror film. We were boosted up into the vehicle since there were no stairs. The inside was considerably worse than the outside. There were two seats up front, and it was obvious that they were meant for the two men who accompanied us, the pilot and his copilot as I imagined the case to be. In the middle of the rather cramped space behind these chairs was a vertical pole that I presumed had something to do with the flight of the vehicle. Since there was nothing else visible except dirt and grease, my assistant and I placed our suitcases on the floor in an upright position, sat on them and grabbed onto the pole for support with one hand and with the other tried to keep the suitcases from falling over.

With a great clatter and crash, huge plumes of smoke emanating from somewhere up front and underneath and a stench from the diesel fuel that was enough to gag us, the pilot got the machine running after only eight to ten minutes of trying. I do not recall much of a conversation between our drivers and the control tower, but presently we started bumping and jerking across the tarmac. This seemed to go on for an endless period of time. There was absolutely no point in trying to talk, the din was so awful you wouldn't hear someone shouting at the top of his voice directly into your ear.

We taxied for an interminable length of time. The tarmac all along this particular area on the runway was cracked and split with enormous potholes. It looked as if it hadn't been maintained for years. We jolted and bounced until our teeth were rattling, yet the helicopter still showed no sign of lifting off the ground. It was beginning to get very alarming as we drew closer and closer to the spot where the asphalt ran out and the trees began. Finally, with an almost audible groan of superhuman effort the pilot got the machine to tilt forward and begin to rise. We just managed to clear the trees. I had asked how long the flight was before we entered the aircraft and had been told about an hour, give or take. From the moment, the pilot cranked up that machine I was counting the minutes.

As we rose in the clear morning air, the pilot leaned forward to what would be considered the dashboard in a car and retrieved some crumpled paper. Sitting on my suitcase behind him, I could make out that there were sketches and designations on the paper together with letters and numerals. With total dismay, I realized in an instant that he was looking at a map. I thought that not only were we in a suicide aircraft, but we were in one in which the driver did not even know how to get where he needed to be. I looked at Maia, and she appeared to be as alarmed as I. This did not reassure me. Perhaps it was to the good that we could not converse over the racket. Talking about it would have made it worse.

We had not been traveling long when there appeared a rather high mountain range not far ahead. Since we had made our initial take-off only with difficulty and since we had not exceeded several hundred feet of loft after taking off, I was extremely troubled over our ability to get over the mountains. We started gaining altitude, but at a rate that seemed to me far too slow to avoid the first peak. However, when we actually got there, we managed to circumvent it by what I thought to be a margin of no more than about one hundred feet. We could certainly see the trees very clearly and make out details of the peak's contour like ridges, boulders, and crevices. I began to imagine what it would be like to crash land in this wilderness. The peaks were covered with snow, and in general, the terrain appeared to be very forbidding. I was beginning to visualize myself wandering around these mountaintops, totally lost, perhaps with a broken limb or two, perhaps bleeding profusely from various cuts and abrasions. Until I starved to death or was mauled by some wild animal. Not a happy picture!

After passing over a number of similar mountain peaks, we leveled off a little. At about that time, I heard a slight popping sound. The din from the helicopter was so deafening that the pinging noise must itself have been very loud in order to be heard at all—or so I reasoned. I tried to ask the copilot sitting in front of me if there was some trouble since I assumed that the noise was coming from the helicopter. But because of the clatter he couldn't hear me and simply made a signal with his hands that I interpreted to mean wait with my questions until we landed. Thank heavens there was no further adventure with the flight, and we found ourselves on the ground in Tbilisi in another hour.

As soon as the ringing in our ears dissipated enough to hear one another, I asked our hosts what the popping noise had been. One looked at the other, both shrugged their shoulders, and in one voice, they answered that, obviously, it was Azeris shooting small arms at us. When I pressed for a little more clarification, they explained that the shortest route from Erevan to Tbilisi by air would take the aircraft over a small portion of Azerbaijan. Since the Armenians and Azeris had been in a deadly feud for years, it was common practice for the Azeris to shoot at anything coming from the direction of Armenia. So much for my first trip to Armenia and Georgia.

TBILISI

There came another time when we had to travel to Tbilisi on urgent business. This time I was accompanied by Tanya and her sister, Galya, who was doing a lot of follow-up work for us when we were out of the country. It was during the time when Yeltsin was attempting to regain some kind of order in the country, following a particularly chaotic and almost total unraveling of basic services. We arrived at Vnukovo Airport, the designated departure location for flights to Georgia. Upon our arrival there, I witnessed the most unruly sight I have ever seen. The airport had been operating at about 10 percent capacity (and near zero efficiency) for the week prior to our scheduled departure. Therefore, there were several days' worth of disgruntled passengers who still had the stamina to wait out an unlikely flight to one of the myriad cities serviced by the airport. At this particular airport, there are no overnight accommodations for simple passengers without influential personal connections.

Airport Shutdown

There were literally thousands of people camped out on the grassy plain located in front of the airport terminal. As we turned the corner leading into the parking area, we could make out their makeshift huts created from blankets, raincoats, cardboard boxes, or anything else they had planned to take on their flight or managed to scrounge from nearby castoffs. The weather was extremely hot; therefore, most of the would-be passengers were in a state of partial undress.

We parked the car and began to make our way toward the terminal. The stench was something awful! At the airport there are, of course, no showers and hordes of people had apparently gone for over a week without bathing. We later learned that there had been such demand for water that the toilets and sinks in the restrooms had stopped working. So in addition to the general filth and squalor many of those stuck without flights had begun using nearby areas as crude outside latrines. The utter desolation and devastation of the place, together with an almost palpable despair only added to our growing depression. We walked through throngs of people, some listlessly sitting on their suitcases; others scrapping over some miserable piece of material or disputed spot of ground; still others trying to sleep through it all. Crying babies, whiny children, distressed mothers, and sullen fathers created a lasting picture of desperation and hopelessness that I will never forget.

We entered the terminal and discovered that the situation was substantially worse. Here there was not even a breath of air or a tiny breeze to carry away some of the defilement. We approached the official who would ordinarily have processed our papers and tickets, and were told that we would have to go to another section of the airport located about half a mile away. Insisting on some explanation as to why we were not allowed to proceed through the checkpoint we had always gone through before but instead were being forced to go to a much more inconvenient location, this particular bureaucrat steadfastly refused to respond. Eventually, after pressing for answers and using the fact that we were foreigners—thus deserving a modicum of respect—she advised us that the instructions were issued because of the conditions at the terminal and the shortage of service personnel.

Exiting the terminal, we located our car and drove over to the newly designated checkpoint. To our dismay, we discovered that after passing through this checkpoint we would have to go another half mile back to the foreigners' section of the main terminal. An added wrinkle, no cars could proceed through this point, so we would have to make the walk with our luggage in our hands since there were no baggage carts. By now rather frustrated, we dismissed our driver and set off for our destination. We trudged toward the terminal, carrying our bags and perspiring profusely in the oppressive heat. Since we couldn't move too fast, it took about fifteen minutes to reach the other end of the terminal. By then, we were soaked in sweat. First priority: get to the rest rooms to wash up a little. That was when we discovered that the entire water supply for the whole terminal had been cut off. Imagine our misery.

However, our wretchedness was to multiply greatly in the hours to follow. When we went to the check-in desk there was no one to be seen. When we tried to determine when there might be an airline representative available we were told in rather curt terms that we would know when one showed up. In the meantime, there was no information at all on the arrivals/departure board. It was simply blank. We showed what I considered to be super human patience. Finally, someone showed up. Of course, there was an immediate rush to the counter by all the disgruntled would-be passengers thus far abandoned in this dirty little corner of the terminal. The only consolation was that there were mercifully few people here since it was an area designated for foreigners only.

Eventually, when it came our turn, we were advised that our flight had been postponed. We were informed that in due course there would be an announcement regarding our departure. There was absolutely no idea of when the flight might be available or even when the announcement might be made. Thus, we were made to realize that we had to be alert for the foreseeable future. We tried to relax a little—which was difficult since the area where we were located had no furniture. However, adjacent to the waiting hall was a small cafeteria where there appeared to be a few tables and chairs. We decided that we were, after all, a little hungry and that, perhaps, a small snack would be in order. We entered the cafeteria and laid claim to one table by placing our luggage on the floor near the chairs situated there. We approached the counter to determine what was available. Here's where our level of misery rose another notch. The lady behind the counter sweetly informed us that all her supplies of food and beverages had run out five days ago and had not been replenished since. Furthermore, she advised us that we must remove our belongings from the area around the table and chairs since these were reserved for patrons of the cafeteria only. We were obviously not considered patrons since we could not order any food or drink. Impeccable logic!

Somewhat dejected, we returned to the waiting hall, plunked down our things, and made ourselves as comfortable as conditions would allow. In another hour or so, a woman showed up at the check-in counter and hung up a handwritten sign that signified our flight was actually going to board soon. We hastily made our way to the counter and presented our papers. After proper inspection, the lady motioned us up a stairway to the rear of the area. We went up the stairs and found ourselves in another staging area. Only this one was virtually empty. However, this hall (really, only a big room) had a flight information screen on one wall, and our flight number and destination were actually displayed. No departure time information was given, but we were happy for what we could get. This hall was superior in another aspect: it had several rows of hard benches and a tiny kiosk that actually had some canned goods and bottled beverages available. We felt like we had arrived in Paradise.

In a half hour, a heavy set woman approached us and advised that our flight had been postponed again and that we must go back downstairs since that was the waiting area, whereas this was the pre-boarding area. This was a definite step backward in mood swings for the day so far, but we had no choice but to comply. We descended the backstairs and resumed awkward poses in the waiting area. We raised the question of whether to return to the city but decided that, since we had dismissed our driver, we might as well give it another hour or so. Luckily, this time it was only about another hour until another airline representative appeared at the check-in desk. We repeated the procedure we had gone through two hours earlier and ended up in the slightly more civilized pre-boarding room upstairs. Again, our flight number was displayed as well as our destination, but no departure time information. This was not a good sign, but we hoped for the best.

And this time it seemed as if we would actually have success. There were probably fifteen or twenty of us in the staging area. An imposing woman entered the room and announced a flight at which point all but the three of us rose and followed her out a side door. It wasn't our flight, but the fact that there was any flight at all leaving the airport filled us with hope. Another hour passed and the fact that we were not once again ordered downstairs kept us anticipating that we might actually leave that day. Sure enough, the same woman appeared again and announced that our flight was about to begin boarding. We followed her through the side door and down a ramp where there stood awaiting us passengers a dilapidated bus exuding the blackest and smelliest diesel smoke imaginable. We climbed aboard and stood with our things for about ten minutes until the driver received some signal unbeknownst to us that caused him to deploy our bus off in the plane's direction.

Catching the Flight

We were looking through the grimy front window of the bus, of course, to see where we were heading and, shortly, we could discern the outlines of a TU 134, which designated a Tupolev designed aircraft with seating for 134 people. To our absolute dismay, there were at least three hundred people milling around at the base of the mobile staircase drawn up to the plane. Our bus got as close to this scene as the driver apparently felt comfortable with, and we were discharged; the bus, with a great deal of noise and smoke, returning to the terminal while we three stood there with our things on the tarmac beside us. We approached the crowd and tried to get closer to the stairs. This got us nowhere until we began using a tried-and-true ruse in the Soviet Union of the old days; we yelled, "Foreigners! Foreigners," hoping that we would be shown a modicum of deference. It had some effect, and we made our difficult way through the throng of shouting and angry passengers. At the foot of the stairs, we were witnesses to an amazing sight—a uniformed airline representative using a baton to fight off passengers attempting to board the aircraft. He was actually beating his club against the heads and arms of any passengers who got close enough to be targeted.

This went on for some time while we stood there and hoped for an opportunity to present our flight documents. The would-be passengers, apparently fatigued from trying to avoid the ardent defense of the plane's staircase by the airline representative, began to retreat, and we forged ahead. We presented our documents, but the representative advised us that the plane was full and he could not admit us. When we argued and stated that we had been guaranteed by the Ministry of Foreign Affairs that we would be seated on this flight (an obvious exaggeration—if not outright lie), he shrugged and mumbled that we could take it up with the captain himself. This important party was supposed to arrive shortly, and we could take up our case with him directly. Sure enough, the captain appeared, copilot, and navigator in his wake.

We tried to make our case as quickly as possible recognizing that we would have only the shortest imaginable window of opportunity. He actually seemed to have some sympathy for our situation, and when we tried the argument that we were traveling to Georgia on business that would directly benefit the Republic, he promised to look into it and get back to us. Now that there was nothing further we could do, we simply stood there and awaited our fate. In time, an airline representative descended and advised us that Tanya and I would be admitted, but that there was no way Galya would be allowed onboard the aircraft. When we tried to argue the case, he told us basically to take it or leave it—this was the final decision and if we did not immediately accept, the plane would leave without us. Galya started off toward the terminal, and Tanya and I were escorted up a special staircase at the front of the plane, servicing the cockpit. At the top of the stairs was a narrow passageway dividing the cockpit itself from the passenger compartment. On one side were two jump seats, presumably for the use of the security personnel who rode shotgun on every flight. We were instructed to take these seats and buckle up, nothing else was available, and in fact, we should be grateful for the great favor that we were being shown. The seats were nothing more than hard narrow planks that could be stowed in a vertical position when not being used. Tanya and I resigned ourselves to our fate, took our seats, and buckled up. The last scene I witnessed before the door slammed close was a disheveled man scurrying along the tarmac in front of the aircraft screaming for the captain to let him aboard because his mother had just died, and he had to get back to Tbilisi to attend her funeral. After a time we took off, two security guards standing across the aisle from us, fat guns peeking out from their holsters, looking mournful and glum over the fact that they had to stand the entire trip while we interlopers occupied their seats.

We had originally planned to take the early flight to Tbilisi, get in a full round of meetings and make the last flight of the day back to Moscow. Because of the chaotic situation in the Vnukovo Airport, however, we only arrived in Tbilisi late in the day. Luckily, we were able to get reasonable hotel accommodations, and our local contacts managed to reschedule our appointments. We had arrived on Thursday, our meetings were rescheduled for Friday, and rather than take the chance of missing the last flight back on Friday, we rebooked our tickets for an early flight Saturday morning. We freshened up (what a luxury to have water!), had a snack, and slept through the night. Next day, we rose early, and after a brief breakfast, began a full day's meetings with representatives from the Ministry of Finance and private industry. That evening our main counterpart and by now friend, Amiran, insisted that we join him and his family for dinner.

A Georgian Feast

The dinner was wonderful. Georgians are very hospitable people and our hosts treated us very warmly. There was enough food on the table to feed a regiment, and the homemade wine (for which the Georgians are justifiably well known) flowed freely. There is a saying in Georgia—having multiple variations—with regard to toasts, "We have three hundred standard toasts and then another one hundred and fifty that we make up as we go along." We didn't get to all three hundred that evening, but the number was quite substantial. After a wonderful dinner and great hospitality, Tanya and I were driven back to our hotel and bid a fond farewell. We thanked our hosts and went into our room where we immediately went to sleep. Our flight next morning was quite early, and we were extremely tired from the stress of the day before and the intensive meetings of the day just passed. So sleep was very welcome indeed.

Aftermath

I woke up around two o'clock, violently ill. I barely made it to the bathroom when I started to vomit uncontrollably. After some twenty minutes of this, the door crashed open and Tanya joined me as distressingly sick as I was. The two of us took turns vomiting into the toilet bowl from time to time trying to return to bed for some rest. However, every time we lay down the malady would return and we would once again rush to the bathroom and take turns throwing up. Finally, it seemed that our stomachs were empty, and we lay down again for what seemed only a few moments before we had to rise and prepare for our departure. We both felt better and judged that we could get back to Moscow without too much additional discomfort.

We gathered our belongings, checked out, and took seats in the car assigned to us. We drove to the airport and though we felt a bit rocky, managed to get there without mishap. Wonder of wonders! The check-in process was mercifully quick, we boarded the plane, and it actually appeared that we might depart nearly on time. Tanya and I took our seats, she next to the window, I on the aisle in this somewhat smaller version of the Tupolev. The pilot revved up the turbines, and there was an announcement that we would take off momentarily. Just as we began to taxi down the runway, I felt a minor jolt to my stomach. The discomfort got substantially worse in an alarmingly short period of time. I knew that I would not be able to control the spasms beginning to shake my whole being and, as we began to gather speed for take-off, I began to gag with what I knew were the first signs of serious vomiting. I unhooked my seat belt and began moving in the direction of the forward lavatory just as we began to lift off. I encountered a number of surprised stares as I moved up the aisle, and these got even more startled as my sense of urgency became very acute, and I broke into a full-scale dash. At the moment I reached the lavatory the plane achieved take-off. I burst into the cubicle, slammed the door and began vomiting uncontrollably. Unfortunately, at that moment we hit a pocket of severe turbulence which caused the plane to lurch violently, and I could no longer contain the direction my waste was going in. The plane kept shaking, and I kept throwing up. The upshot was that I liberally soiled not only the floor, but also all four walls as well. The only surface of the rest room not covered in vomit was the ceiling. After some ten minutes of this agony, the plane began to level off and my stomach began to settle down.

Totally mortified, I did what I could do to clean up after myself. However, due to the fact that Soviet era aircraft seldom carried toilet paper in the latrines, and this plane was no exception, there was little I could do with the couple of sorry napkins I was able to locate. Hoping that no one would need to use the facilities (it was a relatively short flight—just over an hour) I furtively left the lavatory and staggered down the aisle to my seat, hoping no one would notice that I was the last one to use the site. This turned out not to be a place of comfort and relief, for while I had been occupied up front Tanya had had a similar attack right where she was sitting. Not having any place to go to she tried to use the sick bag provided for just such emergencies. However, the same mad lurching of the plane that had doomed me affected Tanya and the result was a good deal of smelly stomach matter around our seats. The ride back to Moscow was not a pleasant experience for either of us.

TRIP TO BUDAPEST

On trips to Moscow, it was frequently expedient to tack on additional stops either before or after my stay there. One such tangential trip was my very first visit to Budapest, which was scheduled for a midweek departure from Moscow. I was to take an early flight to the Hungarian capital, work the remainder of the day, all day Thursday, and half a day Friday before returning to the States. Just two days of work in a new and (I had been promised) very interesting environment; so I was looking forward to the visit, to meeting new business partners, and to the possibility of expanding business opportunities. Additionally, I was anticipating spending a little time getting acquainted with a city I had been advised was breathtakingly beautiful and historically fascinating. I had also been led to understand that, though still solidly in the communist camp, Budapest was light years ahead of Moscow on any scale of progressivism. So I was looking forward to a few light and enjoyable times after a typical stress-filled visit in Moscow.

I left the Hotel Berlin on Wednesday in the pitch darkness of an early winter morning. There were a couple inches of snow on the ground and more snow was falling lightly but steadily. The ride to the airport at that time of the day was about forty-five to fifty minutes—very little traffic but slippery roads due to the snow accumulation. By the time, we had traveled less than half that time the snowfall had picked up appreciably, and by the time, we arrived at the airport a full-blown blizzard was in effect. I left the car, collected my belongings, and entered the airport terminal. It was eerily empty, only a handful of passengers negotiating the bureaucratic process of exiting the country and an even smaller number of local airport workers listlessly going about their business.

At the Terminal

Leaving the USSR could sometimes be almost as intimidating an experience as entering it. There was little or no discipline in the airport terminal, which meant that passengers were pretty much on their own to proceed through the numerous lines necessary to navigate. These were for customs, airline check-in, passport control, security check, and final boarding. Unfortunately, many of these queues were not lines at all but rather extremely large and amorphous throngs of people desperately trying to negotiate the obstacles in timely enough fashion to make their flights. Usually hundreds of would-be passengers milling about with huge congregations of people lumped into mobs instead of definitive lines with specific destinations for customs officials. On this occasion, there was virtually no hassle in completing the processes of customs and check in. Rather than be concerned that there were practically no other passengers, I reveled in the fact that I had seemingly no competition. I practically flew through customs and airline registration. After that, it was just a simple matter of passport control. When leaving the country, this was invariably easier and quicker than entry. A fairly cursory survey of documents, and the passenger was then free to make his way to the gate for final checks and aircraft boarding.

Soviet visas were small pieces of paper—usually a flesh- or pink-like color—which folded into little three-page-thick packets. Whereas other countries' visas were normally stamps placed onto one or another of the pages of one's passport, Soviet visas were separate documents containing one's most significant information: name, passport number, citizenship, etc. Part of this was detached upon entry into the country and kept by the passport control officer, the rest surrendered by the passenger upon departure. With a visa, one had a right to be in whatever city was entered on the visa's pages—of course, within the time frame also entered therein. By definition, a foreigner without a visa simply did not reside anywhere in the Soviet Union or, indeed, even exist there. One was simply a nonentity, enjoying no rights or freedoms, totally subject to the whims of Soviet bureaucracy.

On this particular day, I approached passport control with the same faint feeling of trepidation I always felt. I inevitably intuited that—given the sad state of our country's relationship with the Soviet Union—a border guard could use any pretext at all to detain a US passenger or in any other way make his final moments in Moscow uncomfortable ones. In this case, however, the procedure was completely unremarkable. I placed my ticket, boarding pass, passport, and visa on the little ledge below the plastic window shielding the border official and awaited his (or perhaps her since I no longer remember the guard's gender) steely-eyed and studious comparison of my face with the photo pasted in the passport and visa. Today's scrutiny was mercilessly short; the sharp whack of the guard's stamp on my visa papers marked the official end of the bureaucratic process. I was free to make my way to the departure gate. I was still not particularly concerned by the paucity of other passengers; I simply considered it my fortune that I did not have huge crowds to contend with. Besides, it was still quite early in the day, and I assumed that, because of the inclement weather, a lot of people would be late and the majority of passengers would begin to arrive shortly.

To the Gate

I made my way to the appointed gate for the Malev flight to Budapest (Malev being the official Hungarian carrier). I joined a small group of other passengers and noted in passing that they were all speaking Hungarian—a language I had no knowledge of whatsoever. It became clear to me immediately that I was the only English-speaking person slated to make the flight. We had not been sitting in the waiting area for long when the information board clicked over the data flaps to indicate a "delayed" for our flight. It finally occurred to me that the weather might be wreaking havoc with the day's departure/arrival schedules; so I decided to reconnoiter. A quick pass up and down the corridor past the other gates showed that every scheduled flight was now declared to be delayed. I also noted with a certain level of dismay that there were no passengers in the waiting areas of the other gates. It occurred to me that we were the only ones to make it through customs, check-in, and passport control before the airport was actually shut down. The fifteen or eighteen passengers to Budapest turned out to be the only lost souls in the entire terminal—except for a skeleton service crew.

For some obscure reason, flight information was always considered highly classified in the days of the old Soviet Union. This particular Wednesday was certainly no exception: wherever I could find an airline official and requested an up-to-the-minute report I was informed only that our flight was delayed. After a couple hours of this fruitless quest for information, all the data boards simultaneously flipped over and changed their readings from "delayed" to "postponed." If you could not receive any knowledge about a *delayed* flight, think how difficult it was to seek information about a *postponed* flight—a far more complicated category. The *reason* for the change in flight plans was by this time obvious: the depth of the snow outside had now reached about twenty inches or more. But no one would hazard even a guess as to *when* we might be able to take off. None of this seemed to trouble my fellow would-be passengers. They sat around in little groups, chatting away in their indecipherable language. They appeared totally oblivious as to when or even whether we would depart. I noticed that many of them would—from time to time—munch on something that they had evidently brought with them and take sips from bottles that they would pass among the groups. Travelers in Eastern Europe were always much better prepared for negative contingencies than were their western brethren and my fellow passengers were no exceptions. They had clearly brought with them enough snacks to ward off hunger and beverages to ward off boredom.

Looking for Sustenance

Despite being built especially for the 1980 Olympics—therefore a comparatively modern airport—Sheremetyevo (as it was called) was far behind other international airports in virtually every amenity and service. In those days, there was but one poorly equipped restaurant that was actually more similar to a slum school cafeteria. The service was abominable, the food mediocre, and the waiting time interminable. However, since I had risen very early and had left the hotel before any possibility of ordering breakfast and by now, many hours had passed since I had arrived at the airport, I was getting seriously hungry. Furthermore, the sight of the Hungarians happily snacking away made me even more aware of my empty stomach. Result—I decided to check out the restaurant.

I climbed the stairs to the area immediately above the departure level. There was a very wide corridor there that wound along the terminal parallel to the departure gates. Along the corridor was a railing that looked out on the gate areas, and on the other side were located various service departments such as VIP lounge, transit lounge, security, lavatories, etc. At one point, the corridor width was greatly expanded to accommodate an open area with tables and chairs lined up in a fashion reminiscent of a prison cafeteria. In prisons, however, lighting was so severe and bright as to make even the most furtive of inmate movements immediately apparent to the alert jailhouse guards. Here airport decision-makers evidently believed they could save on energy costs by practically eliminating lighting altogether. The place was so dark you could not even detect whether there were customers at the other side of the eatery. Perhaps this was done partially so that customers would not have to see whatever they were eating. In any event, this was the only restaurant available to departing passengers at that time in history. I meandered up and down the rows of tables and noticed that there were no other prospective customers. Still hoping for the best, I poked my head around the partition separating the open area from the kitchen and tried to attract someone's attention. After repeating a loud "Hello!" several times I was rewarded by what appeared to be a disembodied head stretching from the dark recesses somewhere in the back of the room. This is when I learned—to my dismay but not to my surprise—that the kitchen and restaurant were closed.

I departed the area and wandered further along the corridor where I seemed to recall another facility had been located. Sure enough, there was a small bar tucked into a similarly expanded section of the arcade. I was immediately infused with hope for there appeared to be someone actually sitting at the counter. Though the man seemed to be the sole customer it, nevertheless, indicated that the bar was open since a glass was standing prominently before him. Smoke curled up from a cigarette in an ashtray next to the glass. From all appearances, he was in no hurry to go anywhere and had been ensconced there for some period of time.

Meeting Janos

I sat down on the adjacent seat and inquired if he spoke English (since he was clearly not Russian). He nodded in the affirmative, but immediately added that his knowledge was extremely limited—basically to "Hi," "Thanks," and "Good-bye." I figured I may as well try Russian since that was, after all, where we were coming from and many visitors could communicate in that language to some degree. To my relief, he was quite competent in the language. He was, not surprisingly, one of the hapless Hungarian passengers stranded in the airport along with me. He indicated that the bar was open, so I began clearing my throat, coughing, and making other appropriate noises in order to attract the attention of whoever was lurking in the space hidden from our view behind a nearby partition. There shortly appeared a disheveled individual who had clearly been generously partaking of the very same spirits he was supposed to be flogging to the public.

There was a very strange anomaly in the Sheremetyevo Airport. No Soviet rubles were officially allowed out of the country. Not that anyone wanted to export any for the rubles were totally worthless anywhere beyond the borders of the USSR. So all departing passengers were required to declare their currency holdings at customs, before even checking in at their airline. Any ruble denominated notes were supposed to be turned in but could be exchanged at the official rate only if passengers had retained their stamped receipt of exchange. There were, however, certain other caveats. For example, a foreign visitor was expected to expend a specific amount of currency each day of residence in the Soviet Union. So it was an easy math problem for the exchange clerk to multiply the number of days the visitor was in the country (checked immediately by looking at the visa) by the number of rubles he should have expended. Since he should by law have a record of all rubles he purchased, the sum left over for exchange at the airport could be compared to the amount he was expected to have used. After comparison, the passenger was usually informed that his left over rubles could not be exchanged. But since no rubles were allowed out of the country, the extras were then confiscated. Everyone who traveled to Moscow on a more or less regular basis knew this; therefore, tried to use up all local currency before departure. Or simply folded up any left over rubles and secreted them in his pocket to be used next visit. Or gave them to a Soviet acquaintance for safekeeping until next time.

Despite the fact that all passengers in the departure section of the terminal had by definition no rubles, the restaurant and bar located there posted all prices in rubles and were supposed to accept only rubles in payment. So passengers were expected to eat and to drink for rubles that they weren't legally even entitled to have with them. The truth was, however, that virtually all waiters gladly accepted any form of hard currency. Since I had not foreseen any particular complications when preparing for my departure the previous evening I had left all my unused rubles in the room at the Berlin. Although I knew the importance of always carrying single dollars (as the small denomination cash of choice in Moscow), on this occasion, my smallest banknote was a twenty-dollar bill. To order something from the bar, therefore, and pay for it with this bill was not at all desirable, for there was no way the waiter would have change, and I would have had to accept his rubles as change for my twenty-dollar bill—a useless currency anywhere in the world outside of the Soviet Union.

So after introducing myself and learning that the lone patron's name was Janos, I asked him if he had a spare ruble or two. He immediately produced a couple of crumpled notes, and I ordered a drink. And thus did Janos and I sit the rest of the afternoon, whiling away the time sipping on various beverages and eating pickled eggs—the only type of foodstuff available. We got to know each other as only strangers can who are stranded hopelessly in a situation completely out of their control.

Janos turned out to be a very interesting individual. During the course of our friendship, which began that day and lasted many years afterward I learned that he was born and raised in Hungary, studied Russian in school because he felt compelled to, but became an artist because he wanted to. He was an accomplished caricaturist, a specialist in animation, and earned his living as a filmmaker. It transpired that he was in Moscow on this occasion to put the finishing touches to a documentary that would premiere in Budapest in another sixty days. He was traveling alone on this particular trip because the actual shooting of film—which took place in Moscow—had been completed several months earlier. This particular trip was meant only to clear up a few factual elements of the film before final editing. He felt no special kinship with the other passengers destined for Budapest since they were all from a single group of engineers visiting a nearby factory for some technical indoctrination event. Thus it was that Janos was sitting by himself when I came upon him.

We enjoyed a few drinks, a few cigarettes, and a bunch of pickled eggs together. In the meantime, the snow continued to fall. Sometime in the midafternoon we began to realize that we were not going to depart the Moscow airport that day. In fact, the airport was clearly closed and the only people in the facility were the unlucky passengers to Budapest and a skeleton service crew. I had been up since four o'clock in the morning, so by now—nearly twelve hours later—was seriously hungry, sustained by only a couple of pickled eggs. Janos and I began to wonder aloud how we might secure a more substantial meal. We left the bar and started reconnoitering the terminal. It was eerie; besides the other Malev passengers, there did not appear to be anyone else in the cavernous building. Nevertheless, we continued to explore in the hopes that we could find some way to secure a meal. On our way past the departure area, which we should have left hours ago we noted that the passengers were busily finishing up their various snacks—salami, cheese, black bread and, of course, vodka. The sight only made us more aware of our own empty stomachs.

Finally, we came upon an individual who exuded a certain measure of bureaucratic authority. When we explained our plight, he suggested that we merely return through customs and immigration, hail a taxi, and go into the city to a restaurant. This sounded rather naïve, but with no other alternative, we constrained our skepticism and went back to passport control to explore the possibilities. However, since the airport had by now been closed for quite some time, there was not a soul in the area. We continued to rove about until we met with a policeman-type individual. When we asked about the feasibility of going back into the city proper he explained that, of course, this was impossible since we had surrendered our visas we were no longer legally in the country; therefore, could no longer legally go into Moscow. In fact, we were officially out of the country, no longer in the Soviet Union. We were nonpersons. In answer to our question about where we might secure some dinner (for by now it was late in the afternoon) he simply shrugged his shoulders and moved on. We were simply not his responsibility.

We decided to return to the bar—as far as we could tell, the only facility open in the entire airport complex. On our way, we passed our designated departure gate once again. By now, the other Hungarian passengers were all sprawled out in the waiting area, most of them asleep, some on chairs, some on the floor, seemingly content and totally oblivious to their surroundings. With a certain amount of envy, we continued our trek to the bar. We arrived shortly thereafter and—much to our relief—found it to be still open. We suspected that the only reason for this was that the bartender was reluctant to close up shop and leave all the tempting beverages behind. We quickly resumed our previous seats and ordered drinks and more eggs. The waiter put four more of the delicacies before us and informed us that this was the end of the lot.

For the next hour or two, we nursed our drinks and consumed the eggs—by now getting a little nauseated. But whether it was from the vodka, the eggs, or the lack of substantive food over a protracted period of time, I wasn't sure. By this time, it had grown completely dark and since the airport was officially closed, maintenance personnel did not have a lot of lights glowing. Soon our friend, the bartender, intoned that he had to close up for the night, and we should take ourselves elsewhere. So by now almost completely in the dark, we groped our way toward lighter territory. In time, we came across a police officer, who seemed more surprised to see us than we were to see him.

The Police Arrive

During the interrogation that followed we learned that somehow the fifteen or so of us who were slated to fly to Budapest that morning had got lost in the bureaucratic shuffle and no one realized that we were actually in the airport. We explained our situation to the official who ordered us to take seats and stay where we were. He asked us endless questions about where the other Hungarian passengers were located, and what we had been doing. We explained that as far as we knew the others had never strayed any further than our designated departure gate and that we had simply been whiling away our time at the bar. He then hurried off, presumably to get orders from someone in a higher position. The wait seemed endless. By now, we were seriously hungry and tired, not to mention frustrated by being apparently stranded in a closed-down and vacant airport without any amenities.

After some period of time, two other individuals appeared. They were rather gruff, asked for our documents, and made us repeat our stories yet again. In time, they too disappeared after dire warnings that we should not dare to move an inch from where we were presently ensconced. Around midnight four different men wearing extremely serious expressions—not to mention uniforms—marched up to us. Two of them peremptorily ordered that Janos accompany them and the other two indicated that I was required to follow them. Both of us were told to surrender our passports, boarding passes, and tickets, and to gather all of our possessions. We set off in opposite directions, Janos and I waving each other luck and trying to maintain cheerful appearances.

To the Hotel

My little group of three—totally silent I might add since my two companions refused even to answer my repeated question as to what our destination might be—walked the entire length of the terminal including some areas I would never otherwise have had access to marked "Authorized Personnel Only." We emerged into a cold merciless night. Before us wound a pathway that had not recently been cleared of snow. Although by now, only a few snowflakes were falling, the pathway easily held soft white matter up to my knees with occasional drifts nearly waist-high. We trudged our way along the path with me sandwiched in between the two officials. At least, the one in front of me partially beat down a path that made it slightly easier for me to shuffle along.

In a few hundred meters, a squat building of five to six stories loomed before us, almost unlit, assuredly inhospitable. I am sure I saw the building many times going to and from the airport, but I don't remember it since I never paid it any attention. For me, it was only one more of the many ugly shapeless buildings in the area with no particular designation used apparently for some obscure bureaucratic function. It flouted typical Soviet era signs such as "Forward To the Victory of Communism!" or "Long Live the Communist Party of the Soviet Union" but there was a total absence of any sign like "Restaurant" or "Hotel" that might actually indicate what the building's designated use was. In a short while that seemed like an eternity, we arrived at the building and entered the lobby of what clearly was a hotel of some kind but certainly not for public consumption, at least foreign public consumption.

One of my companions went over to a counter located off to the side while the other stayed with me. After a short conversation, I noticed that he turned all of my documents over to the clerk. He returned and after indicating that I should follow, we formed the same file of three and walked up the stairs. We tramped up one or two flights and down a dark dingy corridor. Halfway down the hallway the militiaman in the lead stopped, opened the door with a key he had apparently obtained downstairs and ushered me inside. He said simply, "Stay here; someone will come for you in the morning." With that, he and his companion left, totally oblivious to all of my questions. I could not help but notice the scrape of the key in the lock on the outside of the door. I was locked in with no knowledge of where I was or for how long.

By now, I was completely exhausted but so agitated that I knew I would not be able to sleep. I reconnoitered my surroundings, which did not take long—the room was about twelve feet by eight feet with a tiny cubicle off to the side with toilet, sink, and shower. There was a miniscule closet and a narrow hard-looking bed. There were a couple windows and a grate underneath with a narrow ledge on top. This was the source of the heat, which was stultifying. I tried to open the windows, but found them securely locked. I noticed a telephone on a corner of the ledge. Since I didn't know any phone numbers in Moscow except the Hotel Berlin (Tanya did not have a telephone) I tried the hotel. There was no ring, just a vague hollow sound. I tried again, first dialing 0, then 1 plus the number. Still nothing. After a brief silence a voice came on the other end of the line. I asked about calling out and was promptly informed that "It is impossible." I then complained about the heat in my room. The person at the other end promptly hung up, and I began to resign myself to my surroundings, including the sweltering environment of the room.

I need not have despaired, however, for in another ten minutes or thereabouts there was a knock on the door. I indicated that I could not open the door after which I heard that telltale scrape of the key. The door opened, a young man entered, crossed the room, and selecting another item from a gigantic key-ring, opened one of the windows to its fullest—about eight inches. Without a word, he then turned around and exited the room while I profusely thanked him for relief from the heat.

I decided to make the most of my circumstances. After washing up I undressed, folded up my suit as best I could and lay down on the bed which turned out to be every bit as hard and unyielding as it had appeared to be at first glance. I tried not to think of how hungry I was—which was very difficult now that I had nothing whatsoever to occupy me. I also wondered about Janos' fate, where they had taken him, what he was doing, whether I would see him again. Although I didn't think I could fall asleep, I felt that at the very least I should rest, so I shut off the light and tried to relax. The next few hours were spent dozing off, fitfully coming to semi-awareness, turning on the light to check the time, and dozing off again. After this cycle repeated itself several times with me getting groggier and groggier, there was a knock on the door. I called out and there was the by now familiar scraping of the key. The same young man who had mercifully opened my window earlier entered the room, closed the window, and advised me that I should be ready to leave in fifteen minutes. He locked the door on his way out.

Back to the Terminal

I hurriedly washed and dressed and sat down on the bed to see what would transpire next. This time there was no knock on the door—just that scraping sound that acted as a prelude to the door actually opening. Two military types stamped from the same mold as those from the night before stood in the doorway. They indicated that I should gather my things and follow them. We descended the stairs, walked through the dark lobby and exited the building in the same silent file of three as the preceding night.

We next traversed the same path as the night before—only in the opposite direction. It was still pitch dark, but I noted that it was no longer snowing. When we approached the terminal, I discerned lights in the distance and could make out the cacophony of snow ploughs laboring to clear the runways. This gave me much needed hope for it seemed that maybe we would actually depart sometime during the day coming up.

We arrived at the terminal and went through a series of passageways that mysteriously allowed us into the departure area without going through customs or immigration. I found myself in the same departure lounge that I had first visited nearly twenty-four hours before. Only this time, there were no other passengers—totally empty. The two militia men took their leave with nary a word; they had simply done their duty—escorting me from the hotel back to the airport. I settled in for what I expected would be a long wait and noticed that the information board exhibited the same terse data I had last seen, namely, "Flight Postponed." I whiled away some time reading a paperback novel, wondering when I might explore for some food, for by now I was starving. I set myself a time of eight o'clock to begin reconnoitering.

After a time, I heard noises coming from the corridor. Much to my amazement there appeared the entire group of Hungarians that were haplessly detained yesterday along with me. And, among them, I jubilantly picked out Janos. He immediately came over, and we quickly brought each other up to date. It turned out that he and his group had been squired—also under military escort—to a lounge somewhere on the second floor of the terminal, an area presumably designated for transit passengers. They were not locked in as I had been, but the two militiamen posted at the door the entire time they were there made it clear that they were not to leave. The passengers were able to make themselves more or less comfortable by stretching out on various sofas and easy chairs and thus spent the hours getting a modicum of rest. They had been no more successful than I in getting any sustenance.

From our vantage point, we could see from time to time how the snow ploughs were battling the snow drifts. It was a daunting task. Also, whereas the evening and most of the day before, there was virtually no one in the terminal besides the Malev passengers, there was now some moving about of various bureaucrats and airport service and maintenance personnel. This gave a certain sign of life to the cavernous rooms and hallways. After a couple hours of conversation, we even noticed a trickle of *civilian passengers* beginning to appear. The conclusion was inescapable; the airport was again open and offered some hope that we might actually leave today. By now, midmorning had arrived, so we thought our chances might have improved for finding a restaurant open. Since the data board still read "Flight Postponed" we felt there was no danger in missing it. It also seemed that the snow ploughs had a long way to go before any plane could land or take off.

We spent the next five hours at the restaurant, which happily opened just as we approached the facility. We ate and ate and ate and finally conquered the hunger pangs that had plagued us for the better part of the last thirty hours. From time to time, one of us would go out to the corridor that surrounded the terminal and amble over to the area that overlooked our designated departure lounge to check the status of our flight. Finally, the information board changed its data from "Flight Postponed" to "Delayed." After a time another notification appeared, one that actually assigned a departure time—definitely a positive sign. We collected our belongings and made our way to the departure area. After the usual delays through security and boarding, we took our seats on the aircraft and prepared for takeoff. From that point on, everything went as smoothly as could be.

We landed at Budapest a couple hours later. In the meantime, Janos had given me all his coordinates and implored me to call on him if I ever came to the Hungarian capital again. I assured him that I expected to make many trips in the future and that I would be delighted to maintain contact with him and his family. When we landed, I had the opportunity to meet his wife, a very attractive and congenial lady who—together with Janos—would in the future host me on multiple visits to Budapest. I had the rare good fortune to make fast friendships with these generous and intelligent people and spend innumerable hours in their fascinating company on many successive visits. And so went my first trip to Budapest, a city as beautiful and hospitable as the people who inhabit it.

KAZAKHSTAN

During the years of turmoil when the monolithic structure of the Soviet Union was beginning to show massive fissures, and some of the more stringent restrictions began to unravel, I started to travel to some of the republics other than Russia in order to determine firsthand the possibilities for doing business there. On one occasion, I flew to Alma-Ata (later to be slightly renamed Almaty), the capital of Kazakhstan. The republic lay in the southeast corner of the Soviet Union and shared borders with Russia, China, Uzbekistan, Kyrgyzstan, and Turkmenistan; it was considered somewhat exotic by Russians. The most important meeting we had prearranged was with executives of a local bank and representatives from the Ministry of Finance. Our mission was to discuss the possibility of their importing special security paper for the printing of stocks, bonds, and other sensitive documents subject to falsification and counterfeit.

The meetings were quite successful, sparking a great deal of interest in the products we were offering. With considerable hope in the future success of our efforts, we completed our meetings and returned to Moscow. Shortly thereafter, I went back to the States. In a few weeks, I was greatly surprised to receive an official letter from Kazakhstan requesting my formal invitation to two gentlemen to visit the United States. Such an invitation was necessary in order for the invitees to receive their special permission and visas to travel abroad—especially to the United States. The gentlemen in question were extremely high-ranking individuals in an organization called by the anagram GAI (State Automobile Inspectorate). One was director of the entire Republic of Kazakhstan, the other of the city and district of Almaty. GAI was an extremely powerful organization, having the sole rights to issue drivers' licenses, inspect vehicles, and handle all traffic violations. GAI employees were ubiquitous: they patrolled the streets and highways in cars and on motorcycles and stood sentry at crossroads both in the city and out. They guarded closed cities—of which there were many in the Soviet days. They had the legal right to stop any vehicle at any time and check both the machine and the drivers' documents. To say that their opportunities for bribe taking were breathtakingly enormous would be an understatement.

Visitors to the United States

I was, therefore, quite pleased and excited; the two individuals coming to the States would have inordinate influence on GAI's decision to purchase or not to purchase the kind of security paper we were offering. Their purpose in the possibility of acquiring such paper was to use it in the fabrication of traffic tickets, drivers' licenses, and automobile registrations among other documents. I did all the necessary paperwork and prepared to meet them at the airport. On the designated day, I drove to the airport with a large sign on which I had written their names—since I had never actually met them, therefore, assumed that I would not recognize them. I need not have worried. Sometime after passengers from their flight started coming through the immigration doors, I spotted them, and they spotted my sign. There was never any doubt that these were my visitors. One was Nurkhan, the director of the nation-wide GAI; the other was Kurmanbek, in charge of Alma Ata, and it transpired, a most extraordinary individual.

Kurmanbek's face deserved a Van Gogh or, perhaps more fittingly, a Goya to depict. It was all planes and angles. He had very high cheekbones, sloping forehead; slightly slanting eyes, and sparse salt and pepper hair cut in what we would have called a brush cut fifty years ago. He was somewhat swarthy in appearance, but resembled a Mongolian more than an African. He stood about five feet ten and was clearly very fit. His face could best be described as craggy. It looked as if it had been hewn out of stone, but with a very rough tool, not a smooth chisel. When I looked at his face, I imagined a gigantic sculptor hacking a likeness out of granite—with an axe or a pick rather than a chisel. I could see him riding horseback, without benefit of a saddle, tearing through the forests and over the peaks of the mountains. I could see him hunting, preparing camp, and eating off the land. He was the most remarkable physical specimen I have ever met. I believed that he was a totally self-reliant individual and could easily imagine him from a century many hundreds of years ago. He was absolutely loyal; would have given the last drop of his sweat or blood for a family member or friend. You knew almost immediately that it would not be wise to cross this man.

Somehow we hit it off almost instantaneously. Over the next ten days or so that the two men were with me we became much closer than I would ever have expected. We did some traveling (at one point were guests of the Virginia State Police), met with representatives of several different companies and spent a couple days at an exhibition devoted to all kinds of security equipment, materials and technology related to driving in the United States. It was all very instructive and a real eye-opener for my two guests. In addition to all the technology they were introduced to, we had a lot of free time evenings and weekends to become better acquainted with one another. These times became occasions for swapping stories about our personal experiences, family, and friends and customs at home. I learned that—as in so many societies that have been around the world much longer than our own—age was respected before anything else in Kazakhstan. This was so much the case that an elder's word was as good as law. I determined that I was two months older than Kurmanbek; thus, when we had a minor debate about some trivial thing a little later, I invoked my advanced age over him and was pleased to note that he immediately relinquished the contest to me. By the time, my guests were due to return to Kazakhstan, Kurmanbek was routinely calling me "brother." It was a somewhat emotional parting, but we promised that we would see each other shortly in Almaty.

GAI Invitation to Kazakhstan

In a few months, I received an official invitation (still necessary in order to obtain a visa) to visit Kazakhstan as follow-up to the meetings and discussions we had previously had. My sister-in-law, Galya, went with me in her capacity of assistant. When, after a five-hour flight from Moscow, we arrived at the airport in Almaty, we were met at the plane itself. A caravan of four officials and very large, pitch-black, Soviet-era automobiles was drawn up near the mobile staircase. We descended the stairway where both Kurmanbek and Nurkhan greeted us with numerous bear hugs. They immediately whisked us off to the best hotel in the republic. The rooms made available to us were much larger and more luxurious than accommodations I had stayed in while visiting other cities of the former Soviet Union. To our very great but pleasant surprise, we were informed that all bills would be covered by GAI.

DASTARKHAN

It was still fairly early when we checked into the hotel, so we were given time to freshen up and arrangements were made to meet after a while for an early dinner. Our hosts came to pick us up—this time in only two cars. We drove for some time, first through the center of the city, then into areas that were rather run down, even shabby in places. Finally, we stopped at a somewhat unprepossessing dwelling, parked the car, and entered the building. We were introduced to a number of people, but by name only; we were never made to understand the connections or relationships between the individuals gathered there that evening. After a bit of milling about, we were assigned seats at an elongated table in what I judged to be a living room. I was seated at the head of the table, learned that this was so since I was considered to be the guest of honor. Nurkhan and his wife sat at one side of the table, and Kurmanbek and his spouse at the other. Two other people whose names remained hazy and whose connection to the gathering was even murkier sat further down, and Galya was positioned opposite them. There began a great bustling about with hurried comings and goings on the part of two women and one man. It transpired that their task was to serve the other eight of us.

The table was truly a spectacular thing to behold. I'm not sure I have ever seen so much food and beverage laid out on a per capita basis. There were vegetable, bean, chicken, and potato salads. There were cut up tomatoes, cucumbers, onions, scallions, and whole radishes, coriander, parsley and dill. Several plates held cold seafood—salmon, sturgeon, herring—both black and red caviar, smoked eel and sardines. Other platters displayed marinated cabbage, garlic, pepper, and pickled tomatoes, cucumbers, and mushrooms. Cold meat dishes consisted of sliced salami and pepperoni, smoked pork, and cured horse meat and horse sausage. There was virtually no empty space on the table. To call the scene lavish would have been a gross understatement.

The two women began silently to serve us from the assortment of plates, bowls, and platters of food. The man began pouring vodka, brandy, or wine. We were advised that the event we were participating in was called—in the Kazakh language—*dastarkhan*. Feast would be the English equivalent that most approximates the word. However, there is the added connotation that it is an extremely elaborate affair with far more food than the participants are likely to consume; it goes on for as little as six hours and can easily last a full twenty-four, and it is put on to mark some special event. The particular event we were marking was my first visit to Kazakhstan since hosting Kurmanbek and Nurkhan in the United States. It became a kind of celebration or repayment for my hospitality, a circumstance that I only ascertained a little later.

After everyone had heaping quantities of food put on their plates, Kurmanbek stood up and gave a very flowery toast of welcome. This was the occasion for neat shots of vodka all around and proved to be such a success that it was repeated a dozen times in the next couple hours. Since I had been traveling to Soviet Republics for many years by then, I was accustomed to this type of activity and had built up certain barriers that helped me get through the ordeal. After a time, the two women began taking away the various platters from the table. When this process was complete, they brought in a dish referred to as *kurdak*. This is a mixture of potatoes, onion, and the internal organs of the lamb—heart, liver, and kidney. It was served in a steaming hot bowl that could easily have held enough food for twenty. The toasts continued while we worked on the *kurdak*. Presently, the women appeared again, this time with platters brimming with skewers of kebob made of the same lamb as the previous dish. Delicious, but I had by now eaten as much as I wanted. Still, I consumed some of it to be courteous and suffered through several more toasts. When the shishkebobs were finished, Kurmanbek gave a signal and everyone rose with the men all going out to the courtyard, the women to their own special lair somewhere within the house. I breathed a sigh of relief, thinking that the dinner was over; after all, we had been at it about four hours by then.

All the men immediately fired up cigarettes. It was a beautiful evening and quite enjoyable just to stand around the courtyard, engaged in idle conversation. It was also quite a relief allowing some respite from the eating and drinking. After a while, however, we were invited back into the house where we were invited to resume our seats. The women appeared from wherever they had been spending their time and soon new toasts were offered. The next dish that was brought in was called *shchurpa*, a soup made from boiling the bones of the lamb with a dash of camel's milk—a perennial favorite of Kazakhs and was every bit as immense as the previous ones had been. *Bishbarmak*, the last and final crumbs and morsels of the lamb boiled with a doughy substance similar to a pasta, was brought in with a flourish that made me think that our suffering was finally almost over. The end result of all this preparation and eating was that the entirety of the lamb was cooked in the traditional Kazakh way and consumed by the end of the evening. That, I discovered, was the meaning of the word *dastarkhan*.

The Lamb's Head

The feast had required about eight or nine hours by this time. We had eaten and drunk prodigious amounts of food and beverage. I, for one, had probably never consumed such a phenomenal amount at one sitting. The table was cleared (except for alcohol), and by now, the men had returned from yet another smoke break. We were all seated again in our former positions. At this point, the male server brought in a tray on which lay the head of a lamb in a completely upright position. I later learned that the *dastarkhan* we had just finished comprised every last bit and piece of a single lamb, and that this was the head of the very same lamb and the last piece of uneaten animal part. The platter was placed in front of me in such a way that the head pointed directly toward me. I had the eerie impression that the lamb was staring right at me. I was advised that this was the way hosts showed honor to a special guest. In a short time, the same individual approached and turned the platter 180 degrees so that the eyes were facing everyone else at the table.

Now I was handed a knife that proved to be exquisitely sharp. First, I was instructed to cut off the ear on the right side of the head, facing away from me. I accomplished this to the accompaniment of some very squeamish feelings in the pit of my stomach. Our aide then took the ear and gave it to one of the guests whose identity remained a mystery to me, but who was apparently older than all the others at the table. I then had to cut off the other ear. This one was cupped in the hands of the same man who left the room for a brief period. When I asked what was happening, it was explained to me that the first ear is given to the oldest person at the residence—as a sign of respect—and the second to the youngest, the fount of everyone's hope for the future. The reason for the brief disappearance of the master of ceremonies was to seek out the baby of the household who was asleep in an adjoining room. Later, they brought in the two-year-old who was contentedly sucking on the lamb's ear as if it were an ice cream cone.

Finished with the ears, I was next instructed to cut off strips of flesh from the lamb's head. Heeding Kurmanbek's advice I stripped off the skin piece by piece, each time rising from my position, and presenting it individually to each of the people present, starting with the oldest to the youngest. I then cut the last strip for myself. I had some difficulty in getting it down, but forced myself because I sensed that it was all part of an elaborate ritual extremely important to our hosts. Of course, throughout all these exercises liberal quantities of vodka were offered round the table. By now, I was feeling distinctly uncomfortable, so it was with great relief that I greeted Kurmanbek's suggestion that we retire for the night as we had major discussions coming up next day with a full schedule of meetings. An hour later, we were back at the hotel. I confessed to Galya that I barely made it through the meal and hoped that I would feel considerably better in the morning. I was not at all surprised to hear her echo this sentiment.

In a minor aside, I was present at a similar celebration sometime later, this time accompanied by Tanya who had agreed to participate in the *dastarkhan*. The difference, however, was that at the very end of the ceremony I, as the honored guest, was offered the lamb's eyes to consume. This I was simply unable to handle and, luckily, Tanya came to the rescue and saved my dignity by ingesting the unaccustomed and oh-so slippery delicacies.

Next morning we rose at an appropriate time, consumed a small quantity of breakfast and began our round of appointments. All went as expected until about lunchtime when we were notified that our meeting scheduled with the Deputy Minister of Finance had to be postponed. Something urgent had occurred that required us to check back later that same day to reschedule. This was our most important meeting since if any orders were to be signed, any contracts to be negotiated, it would be the Ministry of Finance that had to bankroll the transaction.

TO THE MOUNTAINS

Since we now found ourselves unexpectedly free our hosts whisked us off to the mountains, destination of choice as we presently discovered, for Kazakhs having a desire to treat their guests (and themselves yet another time) to one of the most spectacularly beautiful sights imaginable. The Tien-Shan mountain system runs for many miles along the Kazakh/Chinese border over another long distance into Kyrgyzstan. They are as high as seven thousand meters in places with the most breathtaking crests that climb from plain to heavily wooded elevations to sharply rising peaks covered all year round with snow. They teem with all kinds of wildlife—deer, foxes, wild horses, bears, even yaks, and wolves as we were soon to see for ourselves.

A third of the way up the mountain was located a very rustic restaurant with outdoor seating for appropriate days and a large sitting and dancing room inside where we enjoyed many an evening later in our lives. Another mile or two up was situated the nationwide renowned skating rink called "Medeo" which was once the training ground for Soviet athletes, wishing to become national heroes at speed skating, pairs dancing, and hockey. The height, of course, adding as it did the extra advantage of getting accustomed to thinner air gave Soviet winter athletes an edge when it came to physical conditioning.

We continued up the mountain until we were met by a barricade, which was clearly meant to discourage anyone but the highest-ranking officials from proceeding any further. We never did find out what secrets were hidden in the upper reaches of the mountain past the barricade, except for a fish farm, which I will tell about shortly. My hosts then started to act in very strange ways. They invited all passengers to leave the three cars we came up in, then left the road and careened across the mountain to a point several meters away in an almost vertical meadow. At a certain signal, which I did not even detect the three cars started to race down the mountain side. Bouncing over ruts and rocks, they hurtled along their crazy journey. We watched spellbound, expecting at any moment that one or another would capsize. How they avoided overturning, I will never understand. They roared and howled and sprayed an enormous quantity of turf and stones in all directions, came perilously close to one another and then veered away at the last moment. Somewhere around a half-mile down the mountain, they came to a shuddering halt. The first one there was clearly designated the winner of the bizarre race and everyone was then invited to join in a toast of straight vodka to congratulate the winner. Never was any concern shown toward the reckless drivers who took part in the weird contest, which was obviously put on for the participants' and viewers' pleasure as well as for our entertainment.

Following this adventure, we returned to our hotel briefly to wash up prior to our meetings with representatives from the Ministry of Finance. This "question and answer" session went well, and we were left with the distinct impression that they would seriously consider any commercial offer we would make. We then repaired to the hotel again, this time for the night—blessedly, for we were by now tired beyond normal exhaustion. After a light meal, we turned in for the night for Kurmanbek had alerted us to the fact that the next day would bring a lot of activity.

HELICOPTER TRIP

The following morning Kurmanbek came to the hotel to fetch us for a day, he advised, "fully reserved for assorted pursuits." We drove to an airport that was designated for official business only. The reason soon became quite clear. As we drove onto the tarmac and approached a large helicopter standing on the edge of the asphalt, it was explained to us that the aircraft was for the exclusive use of President Nazarbaev himself and never flown by anyone else except under very special circumstances. Near the helicopter were another seven or eight men apparently from the other two cars on the runway. We were already getting accustomed to this quirk, having an entourage every time we went any place or did anything for entertainment. And as on other occasions, we were told the men's names but never given any explanation of their relationship to our hosts.

We were invited to board the aircraft so everyone climbed the steps and got in. It was surprisingly large with benches along both sides running from front to the back of the machine and having the capacity to seat at least thirty people. The area between the main cabin and the cockpit was completely open so you could see and even communicate with the pilot and copilot. They were actually sitting at a level below our cabin's floor. The area from their feet to the roof over their heads was enclosed by some transparent material that would allow them a full 180-degree view of everything we would be flying over and toward. The engines had been started earlier, so as soon as we were all aboard the pilot engaged gears and we lifted off. As we gained altitude, we also began gaining speed. Soon we were flying over the city of Almaty itself.

We headed straight for the mountains on the far side of Almaty. These are part of the extensive mountain range mentioned above and act as a natural border between Kazakhstan, Kyrgyzstan, and China. They are incredibly beautiful stretching from grassy valleys and rolling hills at the bottom through heavily forested areas midway up the summit to craggy and dangerous-looking peaks at the top. The time was autumn, so it was not surprising that the tops were covered in snow. Later, when we lived there for over a year, we learned that the peaks are covered in snow the year round—even during the hottest part of the summer. As we approached the mountains, we continued to gain altitude. At first, I contented myself with looking out the side window. As we got closer to the hills, however, I started to look straight ahead through the plexiglas-like enclosure surrounding the two pilots. By the time, we had been air born twenty-five to thirty minutes we were flying over some seriously high peaks. To get a better vantage point, I moved closer to the cockpit until I had almost the same 180-degree view as the pilot and copilot. At this moment, we were flying toward the highest peak we had seen up to now. We reached the summit and as we increased our distance from it the entire other side opened up with its steep banks running in an almost vertical direction down, treetops pointing straight up at us. To look down at this sight literally took my breath away. It was as if the floor of an unimaginable height had suddenly been pulled out from under my feet. I must admit to an unexpected and instantaneous feeling of vertigo that made me sit back for a moment and close my eyes. After a few seconds, I felt better and tried looking again. Again, we swept over a tall crest and away onto the other side. And again, I felt a little queasy. After a few more experiences, though, I guess I got used to it, and now I began to revel in the exceptional beauty that would open up suddenly as we continued to fly over the countless peaks. Galya came forward to see what I was enjoying so much, but when we passed by the next mountaintop and she got her first sudden view of the dizzying space below, she clutched at her stomach and announced that she would look out the side window from now on.

We continued to fly in a western direction, China on our left, Kyrgyzstan straight ahead. At one point, as we were flying directly toward a huge peak that appeared to be taller than most we had seen up to now, the pilot shouted to me that our Sikorsky helicopters would never get over this crest that reached up nearly seven thousand meters. He advised me that only Soviet-built machines were capable of such altitudes. Not knowing anything about helicopters, I accepted his statement, but I assumed he was right for Soviet-era pilots were very rigorously trained and certainly knew what they were talking about.

After a time we dropped down a little. The mountains here were still rugged enough, but they did not exhibit the vast heights of many that we had already passed. Soon we were in for a real treat; the sight of a herd of yaks moving slowly over a snow-covered plain. The pilot circled around and lowered us so that we were only some fifty feet or so above the animals. Soon they spooked and began to run. Several small packs of wolves which had obviously been stalking the yaks also broke into a run. What a stunning sight to see these wild, unexpected, creatures in their own native environment! I theoretically knew what a yak was, but never in my wildest dreams did I think I would see one. And so the tour continued for another hour or so when we made a long arc and headed back in the direction of the city. Rather than return to the airfield, though, we came over the last of the mountains and landed on a flat grassy spot in the foothills.

Nazarbaev's Orchard

There we were met by three other individuals who had apparently brought the cars we had left on the runway before taking off in the helicopter. We got in and drove for no more than a few minutes before we came to a stop on a level area near an orchard. The men bustled about retrieving bottles from the trunks. These turned out to be full of a locally produced brandy. So armed, we then proceeded into the orchard itself. It consisted of hundreds of apple trees, limbs heavy with their fall bounty. A couple of our hosts set up a folding table and placed the brandy bottles on top. We were then invited to help ourselves to as many apples as we could handle. I plucked one off a nearby branch, dusted it off a little, and tasted it. Marvelous! One of the most delicious pieces of fruit I have ever tried. Crisp, crunchy, and just the right level of tartness. The apples were, of course, washed down with frequent sips of the brandy. Kurmanbek notified me at one point that this was Nazarbaev's personal orchard. We probably spent the better part of two hours engaged in this activity; then were invited to get back in the cars where we immediately took off upward into the hills.

After an hour of driving, we went off the main road and bumped our way over a track that was little more than a wide pathway. In a few moments, we came to a small *dacha*. To our left was a mountain stream that clearly sometimes raged violently judging by the number and size of the boulders strewn along its banks. After a short walk along the river, we went back and entered the hut. Here we were invited to take seats at a table already laden with the sorts of appetizers we had seen at our previous meals. And so for the next four hours, we sat there eating, drinking, joking, and telling each other stories. It would be repetitive of me to describe any more details of the *dastarkhan* other than to say that by now I had learned how to pace myself a lot better. After dinner, we were again invited into the waiting vehicles. I thought that maybe our day was at an end, and we would be returning to the hotel for a much-needed rest. But, no, that was not to be. When we came out to the main road, we turned left, further up into the hills rather than right toward the city.

Fish Farm

After a twenty minute ride, we pulled over to an establishment that appeared to be one or two small huts at the edge of several acres of perfectly flat space. But as we got out of the cars and began strolling around, the place began taking on distinctly specific and unusual characteristics. There was a series of concrete lined pools measuring around fifteen to eighteen by approximately fifty feet long. When we approached the nearest one, we realized that this was a fish farm. The pools were not particularly deep, but the sheer volume of water allowed the pools to accommodate an extremely large population of fish.

The water, it was explained to us, was from the purest and coldest mountain springs. The conditions were ideal for raising trout—a favorite of the populace in general and, in particular, of the high-ranking members of the party administration who were the only ones at that time allowed to benefit from the pools' bounteous harvest. As one would expect, there were basins designated for fingerlings, others for somewhat larger fish, and so on, up to the pool in which resided the trout next scheduled to be harvested. The individual imparting these facts to us apparently spoke only Kazakh, for he would communicate for a several moments in his native language and then one of our escorts would translate into Russian for Galya and me.

Our guide—the keeper of the fish farm—was a fascinating man. He was small: not over five feet six and could not have weighed more than one hundred and twenty pounds. He was swarthy as are most native Kazakhs, had slightly slanted eyes, high cheekbones, and still thick dark hair. I say still because he must have been seventy years old if not considerably more. Despite the, by now, rather cool temperature outside, he was clothed in nothing but trousers and a T-shirt. His feet were bare and seemed to know their own way around the labyrinth of pools since he kept walking backward while talking to us incessantly. He looked like he lived permanently out-of-doors and could have as easily climbed the nearby peaks or rode bareback through the forests on a wild horse from the steppes. He was wizened from the wind and the sun and likely did not have an ounce of fat on him.

At one point, he stopped and one man translated that our guide was quite astounded that our group included a resident of Moscow as well as an American. He had never strayed far from his native mountains and did not expect to come face-to-face with a Muscovite, much less an American in this lifetime. He stated that he would like to present a gift to "the lady." He then rounded one pool and approached another. Stepping gingerly up to the very edge of the lagoon, he suddenly shot out one hand directly into the water and with lightening-like speed hoisted a fish out onto the walkway. Within another second, he had both hands on the thrashing fish and raised it up to our astonished eyes. It was a fully mature, beautifully glistening, eighteen-inch long trout frantically wriggling in his secure fists. With a courtly gesture, he proffered the fish to Galya who found this gesture so unexpected that she involuntarily stepped back a pace or two. Luckily, one of our escorts had a plastic bag to put it in for Galya was certainly not capable of holding on to that writhing squirming mass.

Later, when Tanya and I moved to Almaty to reside and work on a fifteen-month assignment, I recalled the experience at the fish farm to her. Tanya immediately stated that she was going to go to the farm and get us some fresh fish. I responded that as far as I knew the trout were raised for the use of government hierarchy only. This did not in any way dissuade Tanya from her intent. A few days later, she drove off with my driver, Nikolai. Later, I put things together when she described her adventure. She questioned Kurmanbek about the location of the fish farm. Of course, he knew the place well; after all, we had been there in person just six months before. When Tanya and Nikolai had progressed up the mountain to within about two miles of the trout farm they encountered a stout wooden barrier across the road with a pair of militiamen in attendance. Totally intimidated, Nikolai wanted only to turn around and leave posthaste. However, Tanya would have none of that. She exited the car and approached the militiamen. When she explained that she simply wanted to access the trout farm she was informed that the farm was closed to the public, the road was private and she could go no further. At this, Tanya bristled and declared in her most imperious tone that she was here to get fresh fish for her husband, that her husband was doing important work for their very own government and that he was in their country by personal invitation of Kurmanbek himself. Since the militiamen were employees of GAI, the last phrase worked instantaneous magic. Their attitude now meek and humble, the men scrambled to open the barrier and wave

Nikolai through, even doffing their caps as Tanya passed through the checkpoint. I laughed out loud as she recounted her tale and as I enjoyed the first of several dinners made of the freshest, most delicious, trout I have ever tasted.

Last Meal of the Day

However, that was not the first time I tasted this delicacy. After our sojourn at the fish farm, we took another unexplained trip—this time a short one only a few miles. We ended up at yet another mysterious residence where we were immediately shown into an elongated room decked out with a table on which had already been placed the enormous quantity and variety of cold appetizers we had by then grown accustomed to. There were also the ubiquitous beverages, again in no small numbers. Everyone was invited to take a seat and soon the feasting began once again. The big difference between this meal, however, and the others we had had previously was the absence of lamb meat. Instead of offering the most popular meat in Kazakhstan, our hosts gave us a real treat and served up heaping plates of fried trout from the very farm we had just visited. Fresh and delicious and ten times lighter than the immense quantities of meat we had been given on a daily basis up to this point.

When we finished, everyone went out in the courtyard for the requisite cigarettes. Can a host be too hospitable? At this point, Kurmanbek began to persuade Galya and me to let his colleagues slaughter a lamb for us. This time, though, we were determined not to succumb to his urging. With a whole series of appropriate groans and protestations, we finally conveyed the message that we had already satiated ourselves to an unhealthy degree and that any more would make us sick. So he reluctantly agreed to call it a day and return to the hotel. But one last surprise awaited us: as the smokers were putting out their cigarettes in preparation for leaving one of our hosts indicated that we should wait for just a moment. He disappeared through an opening in the courtyard and came back in a couple minutes carrying an owl. The bird was enormous and clearly somewhat tame for it was perched on the man's shoulder without any visible restraints. After a moment, he put one hand up toward his shoulder at which point the gigantic owl stepped onto his fist and opened its wings. Now we could see the real size of the bird which was extraordinary; its wingspan must have measured well over six feet. It flapped its wings a few times before the man moved it closer to his body where the owl stepped daintily onto his shoulder again. What a breathtaking sight that bird was!

And so ended one of the most extraordinarily adventurous days, I have ever experienced. We were accompanied back to the hotel, where I nearly collapsed from the tumult of sights, sounds, and tastes I had sustained that day. Next morning we rose at a reasonable hour and awaited Kurmanbek at the hotel in preparation for departure. He arrived on time and gave us a huge box of horse sausage to enjoy once we returned to Moscow. Neither Galya nor I really wanted the meat, but would have done almost anything to avoid hurting his feelings after the wonderful hospitality he had shown us over the last several days. He then picked up our luggage, I his box of horsemeat, and we made our way to the car where he personally drove us to the airport. After a number of fierce bear hugs, we bid each other an emotional farewell with many assurances and promises that we would see one another again in the near future. Soon we were on our five-hour journey back to Moscow, full of memories of our trip and wondering whether we would ever see Kazakhstan again.

As a minor postscript to the above story, Galya offered horse meat to her dog upon returning to Moscow. The dog—a rather small poodle—displayed a genuine liking for the horse meat, so Galya gave him probably more than she should have. However, she was accustomed to pampering the dog and kept offering him more despite the extreme saltiness of the food. This, of course, made the dog very thirsty, and he gulped and slurped his way through several dishes of water. During the night, he had his problems naturally. He urinated over practically the entire apartment floor that he had access to and created a mess of monumental proportions.

MOVING TO ALMATY

In the early winter of 1993, I was presented with a unique opportunity: to take on the management of a large government sponsored project in Kazakhstan. Tanya and I discussed it at great length for to move overseas for an extended period of time would complicate our lives in multiple ways both predictable and unpredictable. On the positive side was the fact that I would have my first ever opportunity to direct an enormous project, which could have a real and measurable impact on an entire country's economic and social structure. That we had friends there to help pave the way was also not a small consideration. However, I believe the single most significant factor in helping make our decision was the fact that, even though we would be living in a foreign country, we would be there *together*. For the fifteen years that we had been married, I had continued my frequent trips to Moscow (and, since 1989, other parts of the former Soviet Union) which meant that we were never together for more than a couple months at a time. Also, we felt that the move would be something of an adventure. Tanya had never been there, and I had only made three or four trips; so it would be a joint discovery of a new land and culture for us.

There were no easy ways to get to Kazakhstan from the United States. However, the two ways that were least difficult were to fly from JF Kennedy in New York to Moscow and take a local connecting flight to Almaty; the other was to fly to Frankfurt and take the Lufthansa flight to Almaty (the only western airline with terminal privileges at that time). The Moscow connection entailed a small trip to another airfield after landing—a minor inconvenience. The time between connections was about the same in both cases—just enough to get a brief rest. The deciding factor for me was the better service one could expect aboard the German flight and, even more, the proportionality of time involved in the two legs of each option. The two flights NY-Frankfurt-Almaty were roughly eight and seven hours, respectively, whereas NY-Moscow-Almaty involved about ten and five hours, respectively. I felt that the former would be slightly less wearing.

Getting Ready

Preparations for our move were extensive. We arranged for a small sea-going container to be packed professionally and securely since it would not be treated with kid gloves on its way to the pier, hoisting onboard a ship, the ocean trip itself and a long and rough inland voyage into the heart of Kazakhstan. We filled dozens of boxes with clothing, kitchen items, and foodstuffs that we knew would be in scant supply if at all, small electrical appliances, books, tapes, and so forth. We also took along our bedroom furniture and car. Since we knew we would not see the container for several months (if at all), we packed an additional five *huge* boxes with every conceivable item we thought we might need in the near term. Trying to anticipate all eventualities, we sent these to the airport ahead of time and arranged that they would be shipped on the same flights I had booked to Almaty in order to retrieve them upon arrival.

So at the end of January 1994—during one of the most intense cold and snowy spells we had experienced in northern New Jersey in a long time—I left home and traveled to the airport. Tanya was to clean up and secure the house, then leave a week later and make her way to Almaty by way of Moscow in order to spend a few days with her relatives there. Being the experienced world traveler that I fancied myself, I had long ago given up the traditional businessman attire of suit, jacket, and tie in favor of light jeans, loose fitting sweatshirt, and loafers. I really believed in traveling as comfortably as possible and I knew that, on this particular occasion, I had a long and exhausting trip ahead of me. But in deference to the weather outside, I threw over my shoulders a spring weight jacket that I figured might come in handy between the car and the airport terminal in New York. I knew I would not even leave the terminal in Frankfurt and I expected Kurmanbek to meet me in Almaty, so I opined, anything heavier would be redundant.

Everything went very smoothly. I got to JFK with plenty of time to spare for check-in and seat assignment, and requested and received confirmation that all my boxes would be shipped on the same flight as I and that they would definitely be put on the connecting flight in Germany. Next morning I was in Frankfurt where I had previously secured a room for five hours at the airport hotel, which can be accessed via an enclosed walkway, thus providing all amenities without actually leaving the terminal. This arrangement enabled passengers to clean up, have breakfast, and get some rest before the next leg of the journey. I fully intended to take advantage of this facility so as not to feel quite like a totally fatigued invalid when I arrived in Almaty. I happily cleaned up, had a bite to eat, and caught a couple hours rest before having to check out and return to the terminal for my connection to Kazakhstan.

We departed just about on time and seven or so hours later, at around 5:00 in the morning local time, the announcement came over the loud speaker that we were making preparations for landing. We set down with a series of bumps, then rolled jarringly over a stretch of very uneven tarmac in the general direction of the terminal. I had flown into Almaty several times in the past, so knew that the airport was a typical Soviet facility for a backwater community. In other words, it consisted of a couple of extremely rough runways near a complex of low, gray, ramshackle buildings in which virtually no comforts were offered. We came to rest, and the pilot turned off the engines. Since there was no parking at the terminal itself, and since there were no mechanized arrival/ departure ramps, passengers always had to sit and wait for the ground crew to haul out the mobile staircase and trundle it over to the plane. You could always tell when they were putting it in place because you could hear and sometimes feel the vibration as they bumped and banged the equipment against the side of the plane. But at least then you knew that they would shortly open the door and you would be able to deplane.

Arrival

While waiting for the door to be opened, I tried to see as much of my surroundings as the poor light would allow. But about all I could discern were huge piles of snow located at the edges of the runway. It occurred to me then that, in the frantic, last-minute preparations for moving abroad for as long as a year and a half, I had neglected to check what kind of weather awaited me in Almaty. I did not have long to find out. With a few last thumps on the side of the plane, the ground crew succeeded in opening the door. The blast of frigid air that immediately swept in made me instantaneously realize that I was horrendously underdressed. However, I did not become unduly alarmed for I expected Kurmanbek to be waiting for me as soon as I cleared immigration and customs.

Along with the other passengers, I stepped off the plane, descended the stairs, and walked the short distance to a waiting bus. The cold was so intense that even this very brief period of time left me shivering uncontrollably, and the bus proved to be not much of a haven, for it was barely heated. Thank God for the other passengers, though, for their combined body heat brought a tiny measure of warmth to the bus' interior. Once everyone was aboard, we drove the short distance to the terminal where we all filed inside. For the next hour, I was sufficiently preoccupied with the bureaucratic process of getting through passport control, immigration, and customs clearance that I had little time to dwell on the temperature. I managed to collect all five huge boxes and clear them on the basis of my status as government employee (so determined because I was actually operating under a contract between the governments of Kazakhstan and the United States). Thus did I find myself with a suitcase and five enormous boxes dressed for a warm spring day in the cold and drafty waiting room of the Almaty airport with the outside temperature hovering around minus 20 degrees Centigrade.

As soon as I came through the passageway between customs and the waiting hall, I expected to see Kurmanbek and whatever retinue he had decided to bring with him. Much to my surprise and dismay, he was nowhere to be seen. As strange as that would have been I thought maybe he was waiting for me outside. But this presented me with a dilemma. First, I was not dressed to spend more than a minute or two in that cold. Second, in order to go out I would have to abandon my possessions. At that time, thievery was rampant in general and one of the most attractive targets was the airport. Incoming passengers with too much luggage to manage, and especially foreigners, who might be a bit more gullible than locals, made excellent marks. I finally decided to take one chance and dashed outside, looked around frantically and came right back inside to check on my belongings. The good news was that everything was where I had left it; the bad news was that there had been no sign of Kurmanbek during my brief outing. Thinking that perhaps my hosts were just running late, I decided to sit tight for a half-hour and see what would transpire.

The next thirty minutes did nothing to resolve my quandary however. Up to this point, a number of men had approached me with the question, "Do you need a ride?" I had steadfastly refused them all. However, since it was becoming more and more evident that—for whatever reason—Kurmanbek was not coming and that I was on my own, I decided that I had better get a car and driver. By now, I was not only very cold, I was hungry as well for it was a long time since we had eaten on the plane. Also, the combination of two days of travel with very little rest in between plus an eleven hour time difference added up to a colossal case of jet-lag. I started actively seeking a driver to help me out of my predicament. I placed myself right in front of the doors leading outside and asked every man who entered if he was a taxi driver. The first six or seven turned me down out of hand as soon as they spied my array of baggage. Finally, one said he thought he might be able to accommodate everything by tying one box on top of the car, another on top of the trunk. He thought he might be able to get the other three plus my suitcase in the car but cautioned me that there would be very little room for me. He also stated that for all these extra services he would require twenty dollars over the meter. The prospect of getting to a warm hotel was so appealing at this point that I immediately agreed to the additional tariff and said I wouldn't mind being a little squeezed.

Finding a Hotel

I helped the driver manhandle the baggage out to and into the car—luckily a large size Volga—and helped him secure the last two pieces on top with ropes. By this time, I was thoroughly frozen.

I asked that he take me to the nearest international-style hotel. We arrived at a nondescript edifice a half-hour later. I dragged myself out of the car, up the steps, and over to the reception area. I explained my situation to the matron sitting behind the counter after which she summarily dismissed my request for a room unless I could produce an official voucher. She explained to me that without a bureaucratically recognized reservation I—as a foreigner—could not simply show up at a hotel and get a room. She also notified me that without an official confirmation of acceptance, I could not get a room without before registering with local authorities. While she was explaining this to me in a rather aggressive tone, she looked at me as if I were either demented or incurably stupid. I realized there was no point in debating the issue with her and so returned to the car where my driver exhibited absolutely no sign of surprise whatsoever at my being turned down. We moved on to another nondescript hotel where I received a similarly cold reception. Finally, we drove up to the Alatau Hotel—a far more internationally inclined facility—where the personnel were a bit more sophisticated. After a lengthy explanation, I was given a room with the expected warning that I would not be allowed to stay there over twenty-four hours unless I received the requisite foreign registration from the local militia.

Thankfully, my driver agreed to help with my massive collection of baggage which we wrestled off and out of the car, up the stairs and into the elevator—all of which took three trips. We finally managed to stack all the various pieces against the walls of my modest-size room, leaving just enough space to access the door, the bathroom, and the closet. In an outburst of gratitude, I gave the driver the agreed-upon fare, plus an additional twenty dollars, and a carton of American cigarettes—true wealth to a Kazakh cabby. It was now nearly four hours of continuous aggravation and stress for me since we had landed at the Almaty airport. Fatigued, ravenous, and freezing, I washed up in about thirty seconds, stripped off most of my lightweight clothes and flopped into bed with the fervent intention of sleeping the next fifteen hours.

Kurmanbek Shows Up

I later discovered that the actual time I spent dozing fitfully was less than two hours before I was startled awake by a thunderous knocking on my door. I blearily opened my eyes and stammered out a string of questions roughly equivalent to, "Who is it? What do you want? What's going on?" A few moments later, I realized through the fog of my exhaustion that it was Kurmanbek shouting through the door. Somehow I threw on some clothes and stumbled through the narrow corridor formed by my boxes to the door where his muffled voice continued to drone on at a loud and steady pace. I turned the knob and opened the door bracing myself for his traditional bear-hug welcome. Kurmanbek did, in fact, immediately and vigorously perform this maneuver as soon as he flew in the door. Over his shoulder, I noticed a couple other burly individuals who could not enter the room for it was already overcrowded.

In short order, I described to him the unhappy events that had transpired since my arrival that morning. He, in turn, explained that the airport had given him inaccurate information regarding my expected arrival time. When he first checked, he was simply told that our flight would be late. He then started calling every thirty minutes or so until he was advised that it would most likely land around 3:00 that afternoon. Since this was still early morning, he went back to bed thinking he had plenty of time before going to meet me. However, when he called again later to get confirmation, he was told that the information he had earlier been given must have been inaccurate because our flight actually landed on time. Because of his position as "super cop" of the entire capital region, he was easily able to track me down at the hotel. And that is how we finally met up—about six hours later than either of us had expected.

Kurmanbek barked out a few orders, and we walked out the door. As soon as we left the room, his companions entered with considerable alacrity and began hauling out my extensive baggage. This did not surprise me, for I had already become accustomed to his aides doing his bidding with all possible haste. We made our way downstairs where Kurmanbek quickly straightened things out with the receptionist, and we exited the building. On the ramp immediately in front of the doors—in a space clearly reserved for VIP guests—were an ordinary passenger car and two big jeeps. His associates loaded all my belongings in the SUVs, got in behind the wheels, and drove off. I hoped I would see my things again.

Kurmanbek invited me into the Volga behind his driver, gave a couple of clipped instructions in his native Kazakh tongue, and we drove off. Since I did not know the local language at all, I asked in Russian where we were going. Being accustomed to driving me around without ever offering an explanation, he only reluctantly advised that being near lunchtime he was taking me to see "some people" for a small meal. When I had been his guest some three months before, he had similarly invited me to several different places where I was cursorily introduced to numerous individuals—different on every occasion—whose relationship to my host remained forever a mystery. So the fact that we were going to see "some people" did not surprise me. However, on my previous trip, I had also gotten well acquainted with the "small meals" these "people" put on and wanted no part of that. When guests were involved, meals seemed always to consist of massive quantities of food and alcoholic beverages, and took up anywhere from five to ten hours. I explained that, though hungry, I was exhausted and still cold from my earlier experiences, and I felt that I needed rest more than I needed food. He then offered a compromise that I immediately accepted—a truly small, light lunch and then directly to the apartment where I would be residing on a temporary basis.

During the ride to the apartment, I wondered aloud where my things might be. Kurmanbek told me not to worry; everything was taken care of. After another twenty minutes or so, we turned off the main street into a small parking lot that was so iced over it could have been a skating rink. We left the car and entered a low-slung building where he led me halfway down a drab corridor and unlocked a door. He motioned me inside and followed me into a dark hallway crammed with my boxes and luggage. The apartment held a strong odor of some kind of food that I did not recognize. I hoped I would get used to it. I hoped even more that my stay here would be a brief one. He explained that the apartment belonged to Gulya (a woman who had acted as one of my hostesses three months earlier and whose relationship to Kurmanbek was still a mystery to me) and that it was presently unused and that I could dwell here for as long as I needed.

Kurmanbek helped me open a few cartons, then mercifully allowed me to express my gratitude for all his assistance, say good-bye and usher him out of the apartment. I quickly removed my clothes, showered (thankfully, there was hot water) and lay down for what I hoped would be a long and well-deserved sleep. Next day, I was supposed to rise early, get ready, and grab a ride with Gulya's driver to the project office.

A brief word about Gulya. She was a young woman, around thirty-five I would say, and as we got to know her better over the next year or so, cheerful, mischievous, and extremely sensitive and responsive to the nuances of the complex life style in Almaty. She was tall and attractive in a run-down sort of way and had the deepest black eyes I have ever encountered. The devil himself seemed to be flashing constantly in those eyes. She was also the most prolific liar I have ever met. She seemed almost congenitally unable to tell the truth, and when confronted with the choice of telling the truth or lying, would invariably select the lie—even if telling the truth was of greater benefit to her. We had many occasions to spend time with Gulya during the year-and-a-half that we lived in Almaty, and they were always entertaining, interesting, and memorable. It was genuinely fun to spend time in her company. I can truly say that I have never met anyone quite like Gulya, and I am sure, never will.

INTRODUCTION
TO THE OFFICE

Just before sleep overcame me with the suddenness of a gigantic blow to the head, I reflected on the day's events. They seemed like a somewhat less than auspicious beginning of my involvement on one of the largest US Agency for International Development projects underway at that time in Kazakhstan and the launching of Tanya's and my new life in a very unusual and unfamiliar environment. I was not disabused of this thought at the beginning of my actual involvement on the project.

Next day, I rose early in order to get a good start at my new position. Gulya's driver was kind enough to bring me directly to the project's main office—which I would have had some difficulty in finding on my own. So far so good. From then on, things went steadily downhill. I approached the door of our assigned office space and entered. There were some fifteen to twenty people—Kazakhs judging from their appearance—standing around, leaning against walls, and doing what appeared to be nothing. Two Americans in their fifties stood more or less in the center of the room, shouting in English at each other from a distance of some fifteen feet or so. When I entered, there was a sudden silence. Everyone knew that a new director was scheduled to begin operations at about this time, and my appearance as someone completely unknown must have convinced everyone immediately that their new director had arrived. I got the two combatants to stop their shouting and requested a quick status report.

Much to my surprise and chagrin I discovered that, although we had more than enough cash on hand to cover such equipment, we had no computers, writing materials, office supplies, even desks, and chairs. Within two days, we were sufficiently outfitted to handle most office functions. It took longer, of course, to acquire and get installed an adequate number of telephones to accommodate the staff of twenty or twenty-five people. A colleague from Washington had arrived in Almaty to give me temporary assistance and had brought with her a computer for my use. She was momentarily horrified to learn that not only was I not proficient in computer use, I had never even turned one on let alone used it. So my first challenge was to shape a group of twenty-five field workers and a couple of feuding expiates into a cohesive project unit, equip an office from the ground up, and get it running as smoothly as possible, learn how to use a computer myself to produce the numerous reports required by both the United States and Kazakh government bureaucrats, and school myself on who were the main players from both the Kazakh and the donor sides in order to deal with them. In time, we ran a very smooth operation and produced a string of successes that pleased even our Kazakh government hosts and counterparts. One of the greatest of the initial challenges was to determine the identity of our counterparts who wielded the authority to adopt policy decisions and ensure their proper execution and to create a level of confidence in them that our project group was willing and capable of handling its function. Thus, the beginning of work on the program was complicated for me by the multiple tasks needed to be successfully surmounted at work on the one hand and by trying to get along in my private life without a decent place to live, normal food preparation, and Tanya's help at everything from shopping to resolving domestic issues foreign to our customary way of life.

TANYA'S ARRIVAL

About ten days after my arrival in Almaty, Tanya and our dog, Suzi, showed up. They had left home a few days after my departure and had traveled by way of Moscow where they stayed a couple days with relatives before joining me (I have summarized that particular adventure in another part of the present document). This was my happiest moment since touching down at the airport. By now, I was a little claustrophobic, very lonely, and dying for a good meal. I wasn't exactly starving myself, for Gulya sent me more than enough food every day to satisfy my needs. But I wasn't accustomed to Kazakh cuisine and found her meals greasy and hugely over spiced, especially with garlic that I frequently thought was represented in larger quantities than the food she was spicing up.

Tanya and Suzi were both tired after a very grueling trip and too little rest, so we did not try to celebrate much that first night. Her reaction to Gulya's apartment was as I had expected—complete and immediate distaste. She found the quarters dark, dank, and very dirty. But since we were at least temporary captives, she did her best to bring order to the place in the next few days. I immediately began a routine of taking Suzi on long, fast walks before leaving for the office in the mornings and after returning in the evenings. It was almost pitch dark at these times of the day in Almaty, but we soon grew accustomed to a route that involved a round trip of some three miles or so over fairly even terrain. Suzi loved these walks, and they were undoubtedly good for me as well. I spend a little time mentioning these walks of ours in the section devoted to Suzi.

Our main priority was to get into a better apartment as soon as humanly possible. Luckily, we learned very shortly that one of the expiates was leaving the project soon and that his landlord would accept our moving into his apartment on a contingency basis until we could find something a little more amenable that might serve as a permanent abode. Even these temporary accommodations were a huge step up from Gulya's place. When the time came, Kurmanbek provided the necessary vehicle and manpower resources to assist us. We moved one Saturday and were pretty well organized by the end of the day Sunday.

The place proved to be a distinct improvement over Gulya's dingy apartment. It was in the center of the city, therefore, much closer to my work, to the shops and to the restaurants, the bazaar, and—most importantly—the mountains. Tanya immediately began an intensive search for more permanent quarters. I was still very new to the project and consequently devoted virtually all my time and energies to determining how best to achieve its goals. As a result, she was pretty much on her own. She started out by consulting with the local US Embassy. However, she quickly learned that this was a very limited resource, and in order to locate something that we would find acceptable for a protracted period of time, she would have to expand her search exponentially. Of course, she tapped into the assets we already had there, particularly Kurmanbek. But mostly she broke off on her own and basically learned the local renting business from the bottom up.

Apartment Hunting

Prior to the breakup of the Soviet Union, real estate activity as a concept did not exist. The state controlled the transfer or conveyance of all buildings of any consequence whatsoever, and all land—whether empty or situated under a building of some kind—belonged to the state. Therefore, the real estate business that existed in Almaty at the time I'm describing was in its infancy and developing in unpredictable ways. Some of these were unfamiliar and distinctly different from what we were accustomed to, others ranged from slightly illegitimate to downright illegal. It took a few negative experiences, but Tanya learned eventually to avoid treacherous deals and unsavory individuals.

Some of the rules of the game she recognized immediately—all rental payments were made in US dollars only, cash was the sole acceptable method of payment, the requested amount was always negotiable, receipts were always issued in duplicate—one for the actual amount (for the tenant), the other for a fictional amount considerably less than the actual (for the tax authorities), the landlord-to-be always wanted the tenant to commit for the longest period of time—usually two to five years, and he invariably demanded a minimum of one full year's rent in advance. Another thing Tanya soon grew to appreciate—ensure that the people you are negotiating with are either the owners of the flat or at least the landlord's appointed representative. Once Tanya had negotiated most of the details to an agreement and returned to the apartment for final confirmation only to discover that the actual owners had just returned from a trip and had no intention of renting out space. The people Tanya had almost settled with were clearly grifters who had tried to take advantage of an unexpected opportunity and who would most certainly have happily disappeared like lightning had they received some down payment for an apartment belonging to others were it not for the untimely return of the actual owners.

Another element of Almaty real estate dealing that Tanya quickly mastered was that among the few middlemen that actually functioned as brokers some were honest and honorable, but many more fell into the spectrum of quasi-legitimate to totally corrupt. One common occurrence was charging commission from both the tenant and landlord. Another was inflating the landlord's asking price and pocketing the difference. Probably the most insidious, though, was the selling of information to thieves and robbers. A broker who had just been party to a successful rental negotiation knew at what time on which date someone was going to show up with, say, $18,000 or $24,000 in cash depending on the rental cost agreed upon. In a country, where the average salary was no more than the equivalent of $50 a month, a sum as immense as this was a terrific enticement. There was no scarcity of unpleasant types who would pay for information that might net them an immediate fortune for doing no more, perhaps, than frightening a foreigner (by definition the only person capable of possessing such an amount of cash in hard currency). We heard of several cases of this type of information selling while we were searching for an apartment and resolved that we would take appropriate steps when it was our turn to make a down payment.

Interestingly enough, this type of crime was locally considered nonviolent like extortion or bribery. Almost invariably, no violence was necessary since the mere demonstration that the thief had a pistol or knife was sufficient cause for the foreigner to hand over all his cash without hesitation. At that point, the principles simply walked away from the crime scene, the thief giddy over his success, the victim a bit better educated in local ways. Any complaints went the way of mugging complaints in New York City, that is, nowhere.

Our project was well publicized in the local media and usually in a positive light. Consequently, we were better known to the local population than they were to us. What this meant was that we constantly got commercial requests and offers from sources that we had absolutely no knowledge of. Several weeks after I started working on the project, I got a call from some people who advised me that they were interested in finding American companies who could partner with them in developing local business. Since they were located in the same office building as our project, I felt that I could well afford the few minutes it would take to find out what they were looking for. I suggested a time and day for an appointment and went to see them a couple days later. I thought nothing out of the ordinary since we received calls from individuals interested in some transaction or another on just about an hourly basis.

I located their office, knocked on the door and entered when invited. There were three or four men in the room, dressed rather casually but that did not necessarily mean anything since Kazakh business people usually tended to dress down rather than up. The obvious leader of the group introduced himself as Pulatbek and showed me to a seat. He then made a presentation to me of how he could—with the appropriate American resources, both human and financial—contract to rid the country of all its missile bases. I explained that our project was limited to the transfer of small businesses (of which there were some six thousand or so) from the state to the private sector in a manner that was as transparent and equitable as we could make it. We quickly realized that our business interests did not intersect in any way, and Pulatbek made no protestations to the contrary when I excused myself and prepared to return to the office. On parting, however, he mentioned, almost as an aside, that he might be able to offer some assistance if any of our people were looking for living accommodations. I suggested that my wife might call him specifically on this topic, and he encouraged me to have her do so.

A Home at Last

In a day or so, Tanya did contact Pulatbek to give him an idea of what we were looking for in the way of an apartment. Much to our mutual surprise, he immediately said that he had several places exactly right for us. Having experienced a number of disappointments up to that point we were doubtful, but Tanya good-naturedly went with him to check out a number of flats. After viewing four or five different very mediocre accommodations over the next two weeks, Tanya began to get very pessimistic that we would ever find a home that we could afford and where the conditions would be acceptable, and, most important, would be attractive enough that we could commit to making it our home for the next year and a half. By this time, Pulatbek had lost serious credibility with us.

A few days after showing us a really shabby abode he called and very excitedly described an apartment he claimed would not only meet but surpass our most exacting requirements. We were exceedingly skeptical, but he reassured us that this time he really had a gem for us. As explanation he claimed that the Kazakh ambassador to Turkey himself was the owner, and since he was on an extended overseas assignment, he would be very amenable to our moving in and occupying his home for a one or two year period of time. The people who presently occupied the flat—the ambassador's niece and her mother acting as caretakers—were only waiting for new tenants to move in so they could return to their own home. And they were prepared to do so as soon as an acceptable agreement was negotiated.

We went to see the apartment fully expecting that Pulatbek's comments about the Turkish ambassador were as pie-in-the-sky as so many other fables we had heard over the last couple months. We arrived at the assigned location. It was on the most prestigious street in the center of Almaty, in its most exclusive enclave. Driving up Tulebaev Street, actually a misnamed boulevard, we noted the tall trees on both sides of the road forming an almost impenetrable canopy overhead—even in the winter. We entered the compound through a small archway off the main road and found ourselves in a secluded courtyard and small parking area with an L-shape of three apartment complexes on two sides and trees and shrubs on the others completely surrounding it. Each complex consisted of parking garage and entryway to a three-story building. We were amazed to learn that there was only one apartment on each level since typical Soviet era apartment buildings usually squeezed several apartments on each floor.

The Apartment and Neighbors

We walked up the stairs to the second floor and were shown in by Pulatbek himself. In comparison to others, we had seen the apartment was glorious. Plenty of space with two large bedrooms, a spacious kitchen, huge living room, balconies on opposite sides of the flat and a luxury almost unknown in those days—a full-fledged dining room. We quickly negotiated a suitable arrangement to rent and to move into the apartment as quickly as possible—mercifully in a matter of days rather than weeks. When the time came to meet with Pulatbek to transfer the necessary cash amount, we asked Kurmanbek to accompany us. Sure enough, he was amenable to this request. When we arrived at the new apartment site, he informed us that he knew the place well since he himself arranged to have the steel entry door installed. It was widely thought that a steel door would not only be difficult for thieves to broach, it would discourage many would-be thieves from even trying. This particular steel door was triple strength and so we felt reasonably secure during the time we lived there. We also felt that the minor detail of the defense minister living next door didn't hurt matters either—there were invariably three or four burly young bodyguards hanging around the grounds near his home at all times of the day and night.

We never met the actual owner of the apartment, but we became friends with his niece and still communicate with her some seventeen-eighteen years later than the time I describe in this entry. Mr. Saudibaev was then the ambassador to Turkey and held the positions of deputy minister of Foreign Affairs and ambassador to England before becoming ambassador to the United States—his post as of a relatively short time ago. His flat was on the second floor of the complex, the first floor was occupied by one of the most prominent writers in Kazakhstan, Mr. Nurpeisov, and on the third floor resided Mr. Dildyaev, the editor of *Kazakhstanskaya Pravda*—the leading national newspaper. In time, we got to know both our upstairs and downstairs neighbors quite well and frequently had them to our place or were guests of theirs.

Thus ended our search for a decent apartment. It had taken us almost three months, but Tanya's persistence and daily hard grind in seeking out all possibilities, visiting literally hundreds of flats and checking out all plausible leads finally paid off. We were ensconced in beautiful and spacious quarters that were both comfortable for us and a source of pride to invite guests. Of no small importance was the fact that the flat was itself safe and also located in one of the safest areas of the city. During the next year or so that we lived there it really became our home away from home.

One of the great perks of the new apartment was its proximity to the project office. It was close enough that it took no more than five minutes for me to get back and forth. The greatest advantage here was that I could (and did) come home for lunch every day instead of eating the ulcer-inducing food at one of the few restaurants or cafeterias located near the project office.

After a time, I grew accustomed to the rigors of the project, and Tanya got to know all the places in town where she could obtain most of the day-to-day things that made life a little easier. We began to fall into a routine punctuated by work, business travel, weekly visits to the bazaar, and regular trips up into the mountains that soon became the main focus of our free-time activity.

AKTAU

Our purpose in going to Kazakhstan was to assist the country in privatizing state-owned enterprises. This was a US AID (United States Agency for International Development)-funded project and was aimed at small businesses. By definition, it meant that we were confined to selling off retail establishments, beauty salons, bathhouses, food warehouses, trucking companies, small department stores, and the like—basically companies that were likely to have fifty or fewer employees. We instituted a system of auctions with concurrent media exposure and tried, wherever possible, to enlist the aid of local officials. Indeed, a major part of our task was to convince local officials that it was in everyone's best interest to transfer these facilities into the hands of private individuals and institutions. The theory was that this would improve competition and, therefore, enhance employment numbers, quality, price effectiveness, and variety—precisely the things that were lacking under the old Soviet system of a centrally planned economy.

The republic-based bureaucratic entity involved with this process was called the State Committee for Privatization, so naturally we called the regional representatives "Territorial Committees" or, for short, Tercoms. On the far west edge of Kazakhstan, on the

Caspian Sea, was a city called Aktau. Since it was geographically well located and the site of a large population and business center, we had set up a tercom there. On the first year anniversary of establishing the Aktau Tercom several of us were invited to attend ceremonial celebrations that were certain to become somewhat triumphant. In point of fact, we had had a large measure of success in the area, and the locals were anxious to mark these successes in a public way. Since it was going to be a full weekend of activity, both business-oriented and social, I decided to bring Tanya along as well.

On the Plane

On Friday, we were scheduled to depart for Aktau. We arrived at the rather rudimentary airport in Almaty on time, went through the local document-checking process and boarded the aircraft. It was a typical Soviet era plane—a Tupolev 129. In other words, seats for 129 people—small and uncomfortable. The seats were positioned very close to one another, both east/west and north/south. I sat on the far east of my row, next to the aisle, with Tanya next to me just to the west. North of me was a massive creature who filled his seat to overflowing. He was bulging out in all directions. Given the penchant for local air passengers to put their seat backs down to full position as soon as cruising altitude was achieved (and sometimes well before), I was concerned from the very beginning.

We sat on the tarmac for what seemed an eternity. The old Soviet habit of never informing passengers if there was a problem, not to mention what it might be, carried over even after the breakup of the Union. So everyone realized that there was some unknown difficulty preventing us from taking off, but no one knew what it was or how long it would last. The only thing we knew for a certainty was that the problem was not traffic related. Almaty probably had no more than a hundred take-offs and landings on any given day. It was very hot—probably around 90 degrees, certainly more on the runway. Of course, there was no air conditioning since the pilot had not even activated the engines. As it got increasingly uncomfortable, and as time dragged on without any explanation of why we were delayed or even how long the delay might last, people got more and more distressed, fidgety, and irritable.

Minor Altercation

Finally, without any explanations or apology, the pilot started up the engines and we started to taxi. Almost immediately after takeoff, the passenger to the north of me put his seat back down to the lowest position available. It was so low, in fact, that he was basically lying in my lap. As I mentioned earlier, he was a very large person—at least two hundred fifty pounds. With this considerable weight resting directly on my knees, I found myself in an extremely uncomfortable—one could say, painful—situation. I moved my knees around as much as the constraint would allow thinking that maybe he would realize that he was seriously encroaching on my territory. However, he clearly understood his rights as allowing him to take any position that his seat back would allow. I continued to move my knees in a feeble attempt to get some relief. Suddenly, without any warning, he stood up, turned around, and before I could even imagine what might come next, punched me. Luckily, his aim wasn't too good and he managed to strike me only on the shoulder. My first reaction was outrage and an instinct to strike back. But being the seasoned international traveler that I was, I was firmly buckled in my seat. By the time, I calmed down enough to unhook the belt and consider responding to his blow, I began to visualize the headlines in the next day's paper, "US AID Executive Gets in Brawl on Local Aircraft." This awful thought prevented me from answering in kind.

Shortly thereafter, the passengers divided into roughly two groups: Russians and their supporters who were clearly siding with me on the one side, Kazakhs taking the side of my neighbor to the north on the other. It began to get very troublesome. I could imagine a full-fledged fight between the two groups, possibly causing a midair crash. But Tanya had come to the rescue. Before the sides even commenced squaring off, she called for the flight attendant and told her that we required the captain or other officer of the flight crew. Before general fisticuffs could begin, an officer did, in fact, show up and after listening to the sides, convinced everyone to calm down. Interestingly enough, my seating companion in front of me sat straight as a ramrod the rest of the flight.

Without further adventure, we arrived at the airport in Aktau. Out on the tarmac, awaiting our arrival were two reception committees: one to greet Tanya and me, the other to greet (somewhat less hospitably) the puncher. The latter was led off in a totally different direction than we. I was eventually asked to come to the detention room where they were holding him and invited to file an official complaint. This would have been the equivalent of pressing charges, and once again, I realized that our project did not need this kind of negative publicity. I also was beginning to feel sorry for the ruffian who by this time was himself quite contrite. So I declined to make the complaint, and we made our way back to the main terminal where the rest of our group was waiting. We then left for the hotel, whisked away by a sleek looking BMW roadster. Other members of our party—mostly newspaper people and cameramen—rode off in a van.

We got to the hotel and began the process of registering. At about this time, there was a great howl from a number of the journalists. It turned out that while they were in the process of registering unauthorized individuals were proceeding to haul away their baggage. There were probably ten of them or so, and at least six of them lost their luggage to the diligent pilferers. The level of consternation was rather high and hotel personnel promised to do everything possible to retrieve the lost luggage. Unfortunately, this did little to boost the confidence of those hapless journalists who had lost their belongings. So far two great moments in our triumphant weekend. We checked in and freshened up, hoping that the upcoming ceremonies and festivities would make us forget these other negative moments.

Friday afternoon was dedicated to singing the praises of the tercom's successes during the past year. And, in fact, there were a considerable number of them. The local office had auctioned off several hundred small businesses and most of them seemed to be running rather well, which meant that they were expanding, improving both variety and quality of goods for sale, getting profitable, and adding employees. The meetings were very uplifting and everyone was gratified that we were spending US citizens' capital so efficiently. That evening we attended a typical celebratory banquet (a slightly less efficient expenditure of the same US taxpayers' money).

Not far down the road from Aktau was another population center called Atirau. A durable and compelling connection between the cities—besides their physical proximity—was caviar. The Caspian Sea was and is home to the finest black caviar in the world. Near Aktau they harvested it; in Atirau, they processed it. I had a friend in Almaty who frequently went to Atirau on business. When he came back, he would invariably have a one-liter jar of freshly processed caviar with him. It was, of course, considered contraband unless sold through official sources, but the regulation of sales was so porous that probably half or more of the entire product that was processed was smuggled out and sold, or simply consumed illegally without the benefit of cash changing hands. Our banquet that Friday evening was embellished by more caviar than I have ever seen—buckets of it; and that was the theme of the evening—lavish dining and enough vodka to serve twice the number of guests in attendance.

TO THE RESORT

After hours and hours of dining and dancing, toasting and drinking, we returned to the hotel in serious need of rest. Next day, we had scheduled another full round of meetings on strategies and approaches, modifications, and innovations to our original plans on local privatization. At the end of the day, we were scheduled to leave town to visit a sanatorium (Soviet speak for resort/cum spa) for the next two nights. So after the workday, we packed an overnighter and left the hotel. On the way to the party site, we were assigned to the same overgrown BMW that took us from the airport to the hotel.

Since he had a very prestigious car (Mercedes being considered *the* most prestigious), and because he was ferrying the honorary guests from America, our driver led the caravan of officials, guests, and journalists. As soon as we got outside the city limits, our driver immediately cranked his automobile up to ninety miles an hour. It was frightening because the back roads in the former Soviet Union are usually very winding, quite narrow, and frequently unpaved; this was just such a road. Tanya refused to accept the situation and told the driver to slow down. We got all the way down to eighty-five miles an hour. At which point, Tanya advised the driver that if he did not decelerate to at least fifty, she would have him stop, and she would exit the car. When he saw how determined she was he did, in fact, slow down to a more respectable speed. The upshot was that everyone else in the caravan of some eight to ten vehicles sped past us and soon left us in their wake. Our poor driver was crestfallen, all his prestige from being assigned the BMW gone in a flash.

Some of the other drivers invented a new wrinkle that we could observe only until they disappeared around a curve up ahead. In general, people in that part of the world love to race. These drivers were no exception. One car would pass up a second, then a third would pass up the first, then a fourth would get involved, and so on until a kind of frenetic vehicular leap-frog contest resulted. Of course, it was an extremely dangerous game—if anyone had come from the opposite direction there would have been a tragic head-on accident with few, if any, survivors.

Presently, we entered a series of quite treacherous curves and fervently hoped that the other drivers, whom we could no longer see, had slowed down a fraction. We came around a curve to the left and could make out another, almost 90-degree, curve to the right further ahead. There was some kind of commotion at that point—several vehicles, a lot of dust, and general confusion. By the time, we got close enough to interpret what was happening we could see that the journalists' van was on its side about forty feet past where the driver should have made his turn to the right. Just another few feet past the van was a concrete-lined canal filled with—we later learned—ten to twelve feet of water, and unprotected by any barrier. Had the van slid that far, no doubt all or most of the ten or so journalists riding in it would have drowned in the canal. As it was several of them had been hurt. Before our eyes people were crawling out of the overturned van. Some were bleeding, some were awkwardly holding limbs, and others were limping. The toll? At last count a couple broken arms, a broken collarbone, several cuts and scratches in need of stitches, and one seriously injured back—not to mention a few bashed up cameras. We were not surprised to learn that the van was simply unable to negotiate the sharp curve going at the speed it had generated, had tumbled over, and slid sidewise ending up precariously close to the canal.

It was a very sobering experience and put a bit of a damper on the holiday mood. We stood around for about an hour, waiting for an ambulance and a tow truck to take away the battered journalists and their even more battered van. After that, we proceeded to our destination, which we reached without any further adventure. Suffice to say that there was no more racing on the way to the resort.

It was a beautiful facility if somewhat run down. It belonged to one of the local large-scale enterprises and was meant for the general entertainment and relaxation of employees and, most particularly, for the pleasure and amusement of corporate executives. Since virtually all large enterprises were suffering severe financial problems due to the government's necessity to cut back on subsidies, the first casualties were normally the luxury items—in this case the corporate vacation/entertainment complex. There was a hotel-style building with luxury suites to house twenty to thirty executives and their companions, and enough more modestly appointed rooms to accommodate upward of three hundred less highly placed employees. There were lounges, restaurants, and private dining rooms. The building looked out on the Caspian Sea, a beautiful, if very cold body of water (this was early spring of the year). One had only to walk twenty paces from the back of the hotel to the seashore.

Across the narrow driveway by which we had entered the facility was a huge recreation building. Upon entering, there was a very large hall that could be used for dining, conferences, receptions, and the like. Off to one side you could reach a lounge area with bar, a small (empty) library, card, billiard, and ping-pong rooms, and, amazingly, a full-scale basketball court. In the other direction, you could access changing rooms, showers, a sauna and an Olympic-size swimming pool. By the time, we arrived, freshened up, changed, and made our way to the reception hall our moods had substantially improved. In fact, there were already over a hundred guests in the hall, all in an extremely festive and celebratory humor. There was food and drink for easily twice the number of people present, but in typical Russian (or, in this case, Kazakh) fashion, few left until everything was gone. By the time, the party broke up everyone had pretty much put the nasty accident with the journalists out of their mind.

A Dip in the Caspian

Not surprisingly we rose rather late the next day. First, on the list of things to do was a dip in the Caspian Sea. Everyone told us that the water was freezing at that time of the year, but we decided that we had to be able to say that we had been to the Caspian, admired its great beauty and swum in its fabled waters. The place we had stayed at was located right on the shore of the sea so we had only to navigate a couple dozen steps to approach the water's edge. First, Tanya, then I put a toe in the water. She looked at me and I could see her courage rapidly disappear. With a silent "Oh no!" she let on that she was declining the invitation to take a dip. The water was not just freezing; it was absolutely icy. I grew up near Lake Ontario in upstate New York and that body of water in the spring of the year was considered supremely cold by all who had ever dipped a toe in the frosty liquid. By comparison, the sea here seemed even more frigid—as hard as that was for me to believe. However, I felt that my commitment to swim in the Caspian was irrevocable, and so launched myself into the gentle waves. The shock to my system was such that it completely knocked my breath away, and I believe that I broke some kind of record for getting completely into then out of the water. But ever after I was always able to say honestly that I had swum in the Caspian.

After a hot shower (a real luxury since so many facilities in the former Soviet Union had only sporadic use of hot water) and a change of clothes, we warmed up enough to make our way over to the recreation hall where our hosts had asked us to meet them. The number was now down to just one couple: the Tercom Director and his wife who greeted us warmly at the entrance to the activity center. We were led into an elegant dining room with space for around twenty people. It was in the general area of the sauna and swimming pool, but isolated in such a way that you would not guess at its existence. It was grandly appointed and clearly meant for only the elite of the enterprise and their guests.

A Lunch Feast

Tanya and I were invited in and asked to "sit awhile." In the Russian language "sit awhile" can easily mean six to eight hours or even more. We were to take full advantage of the sauna and pool and lounges scattered around, and in between times eat and drink to our hearts' content. The dining room had a low-set window that looked out onto a small, but well-kept yard. The positioning of the window became clear very soon. Two men prepared a fire and set out grilling equipment and materials. The day had become quite warm; thus the window was kept open so things could be passed in and out with ease. The table inside was set to accommodate four, but the number of bottles could have handled fourteen. There were probably six different wines, several bottles of different kinds of vodka as well as gin, whisky, and cognac.

We started out with a dip in the mammoth pool. The water was very cool and salty, and I learned that the water was pumped up from the Caspian and deliberately kept at this temperature. One of the favorite pastimes of the locals—and especially enterprise executives and their guests—was to spend time enough in the sauna to build up considerable body temperature then jump into the much cooler pool. This afforded great pleasure, especially if the action was accompanied by several shots of straight vodka, either before or after—or possibly both before and after the procedure.

We spent some time engaging in this activity and then were invited into the dining room. Meantime, the men outside had been busy. As we entered the inner sanctum, they were handing through the window long skewers of shishkebobs just made from large chunks of white sturgeon harvested that very morning from the nearby sea. We sat down, and after a toast or two, began the most delicious repast I had had in quite some time. The fish might have been the most elegant I have ever encountered. It turned out that they were fresh from the Caspian Sea—famous for its sturgeon and their offspring—black caviar.

Hot Baths

Several hours later, after a surfeit of food and drink, we were advised that we were going on a little excursion to an area known for its hot sulfur baths. We loaded ourselves into the car and headed off. After what seemed like a long, long time we found ourselves in a desert-like atmosphere. There was no road as such—just a wide desert flatland over which we were traveling. The wind had picked up and was swirling sand around us in all directions. It had turned quite dark by now. The result was that I felt totally disoriented. I looked out the window, and as far as I could see, there was nothing but a flat and barren sandy plain with clouds of sand floating just above the surface. Then, in the distance, I began to differentiate a multitude of shadowy shapes moving slowly, but deliberately on the surface of the dreamlike landscape. As we proceeded, it became clear that the odd shapes were camels, moving in a caravan-like procession across the plain. There were dozens of the creatures, and they created an image in my mind that exists to this day. Shadowy, dreamlike, they appeared almost like mythical beings moving quietly across some divide only they sensed the reason for. I might have subscribed the vision to the banquet we had recently finished except for the fact that everyone else saw it also.

After driving across the desert for some time, we arrived at a spot where we parked the car and approached a complex of five large iron cylinders connected by a maze of pipes and tubes. The six-foot cylinders were positioned vertically, bottom ends about one foot from the ground, a dug out channel beneath. Connected to them were pipes that seemed to run in all directions. Everything was covered in rust that that made them look like they had been there hundreds of years. Water ran through the channel beneath them and steam rose into the sandy air. The stream wandered off to a swampy area a hundred feet away. There hung a heavy mist shrouding everything from sight. The cylinders were about three feet in diameter—just right to accommodate a person, large or small—and each was equipped with a rusty door.

It turned out that the cylinders were privacy stalls to shelter people who were taking the hot sulfur showers from the prying eyes of others. We were invited to join in a hot bath. We were told that the hot water flowing through the pipes and spraying everything inside the cylinders was in the area of 110 degrees, so if we decided to participate, we should limit ourselves to ten minutes of pleasure at most. I was never one to enjoy very hot temperatures whether it be a sauna or hot sulfur shower, so I demurred. However, Tanya immediately accepted, stripped down to her underwear and entered one of the cylinders. I wandered off to the area where the hot stream emptied into the desert and amused myself for a few moments with the phantasmagoric shapes and patterns created by the mist rising off the plain.

I had just returned to the hot showers themselves when the door to Tanya's cylinder opened and she emerged. She staggered a little but made her way over to where I was standing. I advised the others that we should probably be returning to the hotel, and we walked to the car. Tanya leaned heavily against me. We sat down in the car, and she immediately fell into a deep sleep. She slept all the way back, and after I helped her into our room, collapsed on the bed and was out for the rest of the night. Next morning Tanya came to—at first quite drowsy, then becoming very sharp and alert. She had slept very deeply for about twelve hours, but awoke invigorated and full of energy. She always claimed afterward that it was the greatest bath she had ever had, and the most restful and restoring sleep!

Next morning, we had the most reasonable (meaning modest) meal of the weekend, then returned to our room where we dressed for the road, packed our things, and exited the hotel to join our hosts for the ride back to Aktau and the airport.

The Uranium Mine

On the way, we made a brief detour. Leaving the main thoroughfare, we soon found ourselves on a little used gravel roadway that seemed to come to a sudden end up ahead. When we got to that section of road, it became eminently clear why the road seemed to end. It did indeed come to an abrupt stop at the edge of the most mammoth excavation I have ever seen. We exited the car to view the chasm which was wide enough and deep enough to take one's breath away. It was truly a spectacular sight. The gulf was at least a mile across and probably that deep as well. At the bottom, we could just barely make out tiny stick figures of men laboring away in the hole. It transpired that the abyss was a dug-out section of the earth, which had at one time held a huge portion of the uranium deposits of the entire country. It had been mined for decades, the bulk of the work being performed by prison labor. Kazakhstan was one of the foremost destinations of criminals and political prisoners as well as innocent victims caught up in the Stalin purges and many of the sufferers found their way to this obscene hole in the ground where they toiled until they dropped. Some died from exposure to the elements, some from repeated beatings by the guards, some from malnutrition, and some simply from exhaustion. But uranium was mined for the greater glory of the Soviet State, and this was its richest lode.

We soon became weary of viewing the mine and, particularly, of recalling its associations with death and suffering. So we packed up our things and settled back in the car to resume our trip to the airport. In a couple more hours, we were in the air on our return trip to Almaty. No more adventures occurred and no more were needed for me always to remember that incredible weekend in Aktau.

OUR FIRST RECEPTION

Soon after I began my new posting all high-ranking officials of the US government in Almaty were invited to the ambassador's residence for a reception. As the director of a fairly large project administered jointly by US AID and the World Bank, I managed to make the invitation list. Since I figured that there would be many interesting people there, I urged Tanya to join me. Her experience at the reception was, of course, unique as is just about everything to do with this unusual person. She prepared for the event with her usual care, putting on the most official-looking dress she had with her in Almaty, hooking a few pretty pieces of jewelry here and there, painstakingly applying makeup and ensuring that every single hair was in its proper place. Our driver appeared on time and we were whisked off to the reception venue.

We arrived at the American Embassy at the appointed time, got out of the car and asked our driver, Nikolai, to be on the lookout for us beginning in about two hours. It had been snowing off and on for several days at this point with intermittent thawing, so the footing was a bit treacherous. Our driver parked as close as he could to the site of the reception, but there still remained a little distance to negotiate. Tanya suggested that I go first, that she would follow right behind hanging on for dear life. Next thing I knew she let out a whoop and landed on the ground, posterior first. She had just been reaching forward to hold on to me for a little balance when her high heels turned traitorous, causing her to slip on the slick surface underneath. Somehow she managed to stumble into the biggest mud puddle in the neighborhood. I helped her up and we tried to survey the damage as best we could in the uncertain light.

Tanya turned out to be a bit muddy in certain areas, especially her hands and arms where she had tried to break her fall. We entered the mansion, and Tanya immediately made a beeline for the restroom. Fifteen minutes of washing up did an awful lot to restore some of her injured dignity and caused her to look much more presentable. Soon she felt a whole lot better, and shortly thereafter snagged a glass of champagne and an appetizer from a passing waiter. And there we were, talking to one or two other work related consultants, in the midst of a crowd. I was holding a glass of wine; Tanya had a sandwich in one hand, the champagne in the other.

At that particular moment, the US Ambassador, who had been busily working the crowd, hove into sight. He bore down upon us, introduced himself, and thrust out a hospitable hand for a hearty shake. Because of the general din, Tanya could not hear anything and did not realize that it was the ambassador. So she cheerfully shouted in his general direction that she had no unoccupied hands to shake with him. I tried to relay to her the identity of the man she was spurning, but in all the confusion, she thought

I was referring to someone else—to whom she immediately started nodding in a very cordial manner. Tanya was signaling her amiable nature in such vigorous style that she hardly noticed when a chunk of what I thought was cheese fell from the sandwich she was holding and landed smartly on the top of my brilliantly polished black shoe. When I attempted surreptitiously to remove it with my other shoe, I discovered to my dismay that it was not cheese but butter that had softened and was now smeared all over my shoe. Because of the solemnity of the occasion, I had on the most formal shoes I owned; so the contrast with the light-colored butter was stark. At the first opportunity, I made for the rest room where it became my turn to get cleaned up. After that the reception got a little more typical—or I should say our actions got a bit more typical—and we had no additional adventures. During the years that followed, we attended countless receptions and other official functions, but this one forever remained one of the most memorable.

During the first years of Kazakhstan's break with the old Soviet Union the United States ambassador was a gentleman by the name of William Courtney. He was the first ambassador to Kazakhstan, I believe, and was an especially fortunate choice for the position. Extremely intelligent, witty and sensitive, he made every effort to understand the peculiarities of life in Kazakhstan, concerns of the people, specific problems of the fledgling administration and how best to assist the Kazakh and United States governments to develop a beneficial relationship with one another. Although he was continually faced with issues that dwarfed ours by comparison, his interest in our project was unflagging. I shall never forget his no-strings offer to welcome any questions or suggestions we might have and his promise to assist us in any way possible with his guidance and counsel.

ALLA PUGACHEVA CONCERT

We heard that Alla Pugacheva was coming to Almaty for a special performance. She was far and away the most popular and well-known singer in Russia for many years by this time and about as well known in the other republics as in Russia itself. Tanya and I discussed the possibility of attending the concert, but realized that the obstacles to getting good tickets would be enormous. She was to perform only one evening, and it went without saying that the demand for seats would be extraordinary. We knew that our chances of acquiring tickets to good seats through our own auspices were about nonexistent. But then, Tanya came up with the great idea of asking our friend and neighbor to assist us with this complicated task. He was an excellent choice to help us since he was the editor of *Kazakhstanskaya Pravda*, the largest newspaper in the country and clearly had access to individuals and organizations we could never approach. We requested that our friend, Grisha, get the best seats in the house that he could manage. When we actually received the tickets and saw that they were numbered row one, seats one and two we figured that they were indeed the best seats in the house and made appropriate signals of gratitude (including an anticipated bottle of vodka).

When we got to the theater, however, and were shown our seats we discovered that numbering began at the far left of each row. Since the first row was directly in front of the stage this meant that the first two seats were so far to the side of the stage that practically nothing was visible. It turned out that the first seats in any row began at the far left of the theater and progressed to the center and then to the right side of the auditorium to the highest numbered seats. In fact, the best seats in any given aisle were numbered around thirty or forty—that is the center. We took our designated spots with a certain degree of disgruntlement and awaited the beginning of the concert.

We directed our gaze to the center of the stage for there soon began some preconcert events. Introductions of VIPs were made, a couple comics got up and did brief stints, and a group of acrobats performed a few amazing tricks. By now, the unusual alignment of head, neck, and torso in the direction almost straight to the right fairly quickly led to extreme discomfort, and I found myself frequently looking to my left and center—that is, away from the stage—to provide some relief for my cramped neck. The problem with this, of course, was that whatever was happening on the stage itself was totally invisible to me. On the other hand, if I looked at the stage to enjoy what was going on there, I soon got a terrible crimp in my neck. Soon there occurred a pause in the program: clearly the pregame show was finished, and it was nearing time for Alla to make her appearance.

Shortly after we entered the theater and situated ourselves, a large group of rather boisterous people swarmed in and begun milling around to our immediate right. They began seating themselves in the exact places we had originally thought we would be ensconced in. There were about twenty or thirty people in the group ranging in age from teenage to middle age, and they were all native Kazakhs. Tanya of course was incensed over the whole thing. She thought we should have the better seats than the ones we were assigned. So during the brief pause in the program she did a little reconnaissance and discovered that the group that was occupying the center section of the first row was none other than the wife of the president, Nursultan Nazarbaev, and her invitees. Tanya approached the matron of the group and whispered mysteriously in her ear for a few moments. Shortly thereafter, we were requested to move—to the very center of the first row, which seats had by now been vacated by a couple younger members of Mrs. Nazarbaev's entourage. It was from that vantage point that we very much enjoyed watching the entire performance which was wonderful by any measure.

Alla Pugacheva gave a very memorable performance and afterward there was a salute to the patrons of the concert, the presidents of the two most powerful private banks in the country. After acknowledging the thanks of the audience and giving appropriate obeisance to the president's wife and relatives, they descended from the stage. In front of the entire audience and right next to the Nazarbaev family, they approached me, shook my hand, and asked how I had enjoyed the concert. I answered that it had been terrific and introduced them to my wife. I then mentioned that we would have enjoyed the concert far less had it not been for the generosity of the Nazarbaev clan. This seemed to impress the bank presidents no end for they automatically assumed that Tanya and I were on close terms with the Nazarbaev family. On the other hand, I could sense that Mrs. Nazarbaev was impressed with the high-business standing of my acquaintances. I saw no reason to explain to the bank presidents the circumstances of our involvement with the Nazarbaev family, nor to Mrs. Nazarbaev the fact that I had simply met the bank executives in the normal course of work in directing the USAID project on privatization. And so it was that Tanya and I enjoyed our one and only Pugacheva concert from the best seats in the house and then appeared to be giants of Almaty's business and social class in the eyes of the other theater-goers.

SUZI

In a slight departure from my chosen format, that is, to narrate some of the adventures and experiences that made my travel and work in Russia and the Soviet Union so memorable—I would like briefly to recount our acquisition of and subsequent life with the dog that became our beloved pet for life. Since she played such a prominent role in our stay overseas, our early relationship with her before moving from the States will help explain what kind of dog she was, and how important she was to our family life while abroad. The dog was so much a part of our lives that this journal would be considerably poorer and less interesting without mention of her.

So Tanya and I decided to get a dog. It happened this way—our son Greg was staying with friends in the northwestern part of New Jersey. Not far was a farm and somehow Greg found out that the residents' Doberman had recently had a litter. I saw them once when up on a visit to Greg and thought they were real pretty pups and so suggested to Tanya that we obtain one. I had grown up in a family where we always had dogs, so it seemed like the natural thing to do. She agreed, despite the fact that she had never had a dog and consequently did not realize how much bother they could be. She learned later. In any event, we decided to get a dog.

Getting a Dog

On the fateful day, Tanya came with me to pick out our new pet. We went to the farm and were immediately attacked by a very *large* and seemingly fierce Doberman. I had almost got out of the car when this beast came tearing out of the barn. I barely made it back into the car by the time the animal got there. After our repeated calls for help, the owner mercifully called the dog off and secured it to the barn with a stout piece of rope. We got out of the car and ambled over to where we could see the pups were kept. They were beautiful dogs, and we had no trouble in selecting one. They were no longer puppies at a couple of months old; and were very small for Dobermans but extremely sleek and elegant looking.

We got Suzi—as we would call her from then on—into the car and left for our seventy-five-minute trip back to our home. Tanya was very solicitous from the very beginning. She covered the back seat of the car with a blanket, and we installed Suzi there for the ride. After a short time, we began to hear huffing and chuffing sounds from the back. Sure enough, it was Suzi upchucking on the occasion of her very first car ride, which made the remaining one-hour ride extremely unpleasant. But there was nothing to do, so we continued home. By the time, we got there we figured that Suzi had expelled all the foul matter she had inside her, so it would be safe to take her inside the house.

Suzi at Home

We came in through the garage. This way into the house led through a utility room, past the family room, and up a staircase to the main living area. When we arrived, we led the dog into the house to the bottom of the stairs. Halfway up, we stopped and looked back; Suzi was still standing at the foot of the stairs, trembling. We returned to urge her to follow. However, she thrust her front legs out in front of her and dug her toenails into the carpet with sufficient resolve that it appeared it would be difficult to dislodge her. It suddenly occurred to us that she had never climbed stairs before and was terrified of this brand-new and unfamiliar menace to her normal rituals. We had to put one of her feet before the other and literally force her to climb the stairs. But she did learn quickly after that and was soon tearing up and down the stairs like a whirlwind.

Indeed, that became one of the great pleasures in her life—a kind of nifty game to see how fast she could negotiate the staircase from top to bottom. There was a landing halfway up and a 360-degree turn. This was only an extra challenge for Suzi, one that she eventually very much relished. She could dash up the first half of the stairs, then have two options—turn almost 360 degrees and continue up the second half, or turn a complete circle and rush back down the steps she had just ascended. She got to love the latter particularly since when she hit the floor at the bottom, she would launch herself onto a throw rug there and skid across the floor much the way as kids we used to run to pick up speed when approaching a frozen puddle in the winter to see how far we could skid across. However, we had to control this game within certain limitations. Across the floor from the stairs was a pair of sliding glass doors leading to an outside patio. If Suzi hit the rug with too much gusto she could easily slide all the way across the room and crash into the glass doors—with considerable momentum.

Suzi was not big for a Doberman, but she was very pretty, sleek, and graceful, and she had the gentlest nature of any dog I have ever known (and there have been plenty). When our very small niece would come for visits, Suzi would roll over on her back on the floor and let Julie lay her head right on her stomach. She loved people and would try to do everything in her power to make them love her back. She was usually successful. If it's possible to use the word *kind* with respect to dogs, Suzi was the kindest dog ever. She was also the smartest dog I have ever come across. But her intelligence was tinged with a healthy dose of cunning. She loved to eat more than anything else—except possibly be stroked by a human (particularly Tanya or myself), and she loved to go outside for a run. She would be so torn if she were offered something to eat when it was time to go out, not knowing whether to stay and to eat (her very favorite activity) or go out for a tear around the block. Of course, maybe she had it figured out—that she would get to eat anyway, so go run some of the demons out of her.

Suzi hated the snow! When the ground was bare, she raced around like a wind-up toy that was seriously over wound—nonstop. When there was snow on the ground, she would dance like a ballerina, skipping, and mincing along in slow motion. She would try to keep her feet out of the snow as much as possible, which meant that she would often stand on three feet only, holding the fourth in an awkward, upright position. But holding one foot aloft is apparently difficult for a dog. So she would hold up one and then switch to another, then hop to a third, and so on. When it came time to urinate—the main reason for her to be outside (other than to exercise—which she would avoid like the plague in the snow)—she would squat down to do her thing. However, that was far worse than just standing or walking slowly for she would willy-nilly have to dip the entire lower part of her belly into the snow, including her sensitive private parts. Thus, it frequently took her half-a-dozen attempts before she was successful in emptying her bladder. But the cold was an important part of our winters in Kazakhstan and Russia. Luckily, though there were normally no high drifts of snow, but rather beaten-down and walked-upon areas that were totally covered in dirty ice. These presented no problem for Suzi who was extremely sure-footed. I, on the other hand, had serious problems maintaining my balance on the precarious surface. So whereas our twice daily walks (runs?) were very pleasurable for Suzi, they were very challenging to me. But, more of this later.

Suzi was very devoted to both Tanya and me. But this devotion led sometimes to vindictiveness. I frequently traveled in those days and would be away for weeks at a time. Suzi would not only miss me terribly, but also get very infuriated with me. When I returned home, her first reaction would be ecstasy. She would whirl around me like a spinning dervish, dashing, and gyrating about my feet, whining, shrieking, and howling like a demon. She would get so excited that no amount of stroking would calm her down. After some five minutes of this naked display of affection, she would seem to come to herself and realize that this was not a dignified way to show her displeasure over my abandonment of her. At this point, she would—in the most demonstrative way possible—leave me and go off to a nearby corner to sulk. For the next couple hours, she would ignore me completely, and she would make me plead with her to approach. This would be her revenge for my leaving her. After a while, she would relent and come reluctantly over to allow me to scratch her behind the ears. At this point, I would know that I had been forgiven. And at this point, she would once again become her gentle, complacent self-practically purring with happiness and satisfaction.

On those few occasions when Tanya and I went away together, we were forced to give Suzi over to someone else for safekeeping. This she hated! And this was when she became most vindictive. In the car on the way home, she would be surly to the point that she would not even look at us. When we got home, she would have nothing to do with us. After the first few instances of this experience, we became accustomed to what awaited us—a large neat and steaming pile of excrement in the middle of the living room floor. Suzi would wait until we were least expecting it then sneak off to the other room and leave her measure of discontent. That it was deliberate I never had the slightest doubt. I have never heard of a more obvious indication of an animal's desire for payback.

Suzi and Tanya had a very special relationship. Tanya was very fond of and devoted to the dog, and Suzi, in turn, simply adored Tanya. However, there was one major caveat; regardless of how sternly Tanya gave orders to Suzi, the dog paid her absolutely no mind. It was almost as if she had made a conscious determination to accept instructions only from me, and since she followed all my orders unequivocally (except not to run away outside) felt that she had no obligation whatsoever to obey Tanya. But Tanya was the one who prepared her food, and this elicited a huge amount of respect from Suzi. When not engaged in some other activity, Tanya typically occupied herself in the kitchen, usually at the counter. The height here was just right for Suzi; she could approach Tanya, fit her snout perfectly under Tanya's elbow and start jiggling. Tanya was such a softy that she would frequently toss Suzi some morsel. Before ever cooking our dinner, Tanya would always prepare the dog's repast. This was often an elaborate mixture of nutritious ingredients making up a kind of soup or stew that usually smelled so delicious that I wouldn't have minded trying it myself. It would then be my chore to take this concoction to the designated corner where Suzi's eating area was located. This was because she attacked her food with such a ferocious intensity that bits and pieces of it would go flying off in all directions. At least this way, Tanya could keep the devastation confined. This was also where I gave Suzi lessons in obedience. I would sit her down three feet away from her eating place, place the bowl on the floor, and tell her to wait. Quivering in anticipation, she would direct her unwavering attention now toward me, now at the bowl waiting for the signal that would allow her to eat. This would come after I took a few moments soothing her with words like, "Where's your bowl, Suzi?" or, "Just another minute, Suzi," or "Boy, that smells good, girl." Then I would mouth a somewhat louder and very authoritarian, "OK!" at which point she would make a great leap toward her bowl. I swear that she began masticating even before she reached it so that she was in full swing by the time her lips and teeth actually touched the food.

Suzi's Trip to Moscow

Prior to 1994, I had conducted my business in the Soviet Union at long distance, that is, I had simply boarded a plane and visited the country whenever it was required—on average every two months or so—and for as long as was necessary—usually a few weeks at a time. In the winter of 1993, I was offered a position as director of a joint US government and World Bank program to privatize small businesses in Kazakhstan, one of the newly formed states that arose out of the ashes of the fifteen former Soviet republics. The job would be substantially different from what I had been engaged in, and it would necessitate my living abroad for at least a year-and-a-half with no out-of-country travel for more than a week at a time for each six-month period. I would be housed in-country for the duration of the project.

Tanya and I talked about it in considerable detail for it would mean uprooting our family completely for at least a year and a half and living in an environment that neither of us was accustomed to. Not the least of our worries was Suzi. However, we did not debate for long. She was almost as much a member of our family as Tanya and I. But there were considerable logistics to work out.

When we decided to take Suzi to Kazakhstan with us, we went out and bought the largest individual kennel we could find. It was lightweight plastic and measured approximately three by two by three feet high. Since she was not a particularly large dog to begin with she fit inside pretty easily. When it came close to the time we were supposed to leave for Alma Ata, as the capital of Kazakhstan was then called, we checked with the veterinarian on the best way to accomplish her transport. We explained that the flight to Moscow was around nine to ten hours, and the onward flight to Alma Ata about another five. Tanya and Suzi planned to spend two to three days in Moscow visiting family and, in general, recuperating a little for the second leg of the trip. The vet gave us (I should say sold us for an extraordinary amount of money!) several types and kinds of medication (mostly various sedatives to keep Suzi settled down). Since I had to leave for Kazakhstan a week earlier, it was up to Tanya to administer the drugs. She really gave Suzi a good dose, both before leaving for the airport, and once again, just before checking her in with the rest of the baggage. So Suzi was already pretty groggy when Tanya gave her the second dose upon check-in. After that, she knew nothing more until disembarking in Moscow some ten to twelve hours later.

Suzi's Arrival

In those days, the procedure for passing through passport control in the main Moscow airport (called Sheremetyevo) was nothing less than hell. It usually took well over an hour—sometimes considerably more. By the time Tanya cleared passport inspection formalities, therefore, her baggage was already endlessly circling on the ancient and creaky carousel. All of her many suitcases, but no Suzi! Tanya immediately became very nervous when Suzi's absence continued. After some time it became obvious that Suzi's kennel was not going to be placed on the carousel with the rest of the luggage. By the time all the other passengers had received their baggage and left the hall, Tanya had become frantic. She began looking for anyone who could check the other side of the wall of the baggage retrieval area to see if, inadvertently, Suzi and her kennel had been left behind. Most of the workmen she pleaded with had no interest in helping. Finally, after the offering of a considerable financial reward (half up front, of course), one individual offered to look out on the tarmac behind the luggage carousel.

Ten minutes after he left Tanya nervously waiting at the baggage carousel he returned with the kennel in tow. All Tanya could see was the outline of the kennel itself and a mass of blackness on its floor. When she managed to get the complicated door unlocked and opened, she expected that Suzi would immediately emerge. She did not. Tanya reached inside to prod Suzi a little and felt the coldest animal she had ever touched. She had to wrestle Suzi out of the kennel—a not entirely simple feat despite Suzi's relative small size. She was, after all lying in a completely prone position, absolutely unable to move anything herself. And, of course, Tanya had to pull out the dog while kneeling on the floor and bending her whole body forward without any leverage. She pushed and prodded, shoved and nudged until she finally got Suzi wrestled out of the kennel.

Suzi was a helpless bundle of frozen limbs and joints. All she was capable of doing was trembling. She shivered and shook from nose to the tip of her tail. She coughed and wheezed and rolled her eyes. Tanya was sure that the dog was expiring in front of her eyes. She screamed for some help and finally, one baggage handler proffered a ratty old blanket—which, of course, Tanya had promptly to pay for. She did not even begrudge the fact that she gave the man enough cash to buy several new blankets. Wrapping Suzi up in the smelly piece of fabric as best she could Tanya then tried to negotiate the dog plus all her luggage through customs. It goes without saying that this also cost a neat piece of change, but at least Tanya could be sure that help would be waiting on the other side of customs, for her sister was certain to meet her there. She later calculated that Suzi was outside on the airport tarmac for over an hour—in minus 20 degree temperatures. By the time, the plane landed Suzi was sure to have recovered from the drugs and been wide-awake for quite some time. So she would have been one seriously hungry, freezing, and terrified animal.

Tanya's sister and brother-in-law whisked her, Suzi, and the luggage home. By the time they got there, Tanya was exhausted—jet lag, eight hours' time difference, her fears for the dog, and the normal stress and strain of a long trip—nearly twenty hours since she left home. Suzi, on the other hand, was practically comatose, still absolutely unable to move a muscle and completely a-tremble from head to toe. After a few days of lounging around the warm apartment in Moscow, however, Suzi shook off the effects of her traumatic trip and became her old frisky self again.

Suzi's Life in Almaty

In Almaty (after the Kazakhization of the former Alma Ata), then later in Moscow, Suzi got in the habit of sleeping in the bottom portion of her kennel. The front of this section was scooped down to about three inches above the floor so we could always see her. And whenever she would look up she would see right over the lowered front end. Whenever either Tanya or I were up and about, Suzi would always be with us. If we were both absent, she would always get in the kennel to wait for us. But when we were present in the apartment, Suzi would always be in the same room either quietly waiting for attention or actively seeking it.

Suzi's most hated time was bath day. It was the only time that she would get in the kennel when we were around. As soon as she heard that abominable word *bath* or *mytsya*, (the Russian word for wash) she would slink off to her room and curl up in the kennel, cringing as if the devil himself was after her. Normally, she would curl up with hindquarters to the wall, head propped on her front paws, looking into the room. On bath day, her gaze would studiously avoid us—like a poor elementary school student doing everything to avoid his teacher's glance in an attempt to have her focus on someone else to pose whatever question she had in mind. Suzi would try to make herself as small as possible—maybe we wouldn't notice her?

But we were adamant when it came to washing Suzi. Having warned her of the impending unpleasant experience, we would go to fetch her, almost physically drag her to the bathroom and hoist her into the bathtub. At moments like these, I was always very thankful that she was not a particularly large Doberman. Since she weighed comparatively little, I could manhandle her into the tub with relative ease despite her flailing legs and frantic wriggling about. We would get her into the tub; Tanya would splash some water on her and begin to lather her up. Then she would rinse the dog, lather her again, and rinse her another time or two. During all this activity, Suzi would sit on her rear, front legs rigid from shoulders to toes, looking straight ahead, and trembling in every joint and muscle. She absolutely loathed the process. However, when she was more or less dried off and let free, she would jump and prance around the apartment as if she were a three-month-old pup being offered the chance to run free for the first time ever. She would bark a little and make her feeble efforts at smiling, happy as a lark to have the ordeal over yet another time.

Going for Walks

Suzi and I would go walking every day, usually early in the morning. I say walk but, in fact, our gait was more like a trot. As soon as we hit the outdoors, she would get into her stride. All four legs moving as fast as I would let her go, she would be straining at the leash. It was like a rope drawn to fullest length, looking for all the world as if it would break at any moment. On cold winter days, when the temperature was frequently in the minus column of double digits Suzi would somehow bring to mind a sleek, black-skinned dragon. Exerting every muscle in her compact body, she would move down the sidewalk, every couple seconds or so moving her head from right to left then back again. As she would move, the steam would come out of her nostrils pluming the air with thick clouds of condensed mist. Since she was straining so hard, the air puffs were thick and long, like the steam escaping from a nineteenth century locomotive. She did, indeed, look like a dragon, huffing and puffing smoke in all directions.

In Almaty, they didn't have the snow removal equipment we were accustomed to. In general, they cleaned the streets on only a semi regular basis and the sidewalks not at all. Since it snowed fairly often, it would build up on the areas that weren't cleared, get packed down then covered over once again. The result was that during the entire course of the winter accumulated snow, trampled into dirty ice, would raise the level of the walkways by a factor of twenty inches or more. It was on such sidewalks that Suzi and I would get our morning exercise. Somehow, the raising of the level on which we trotted seemed also to raise Suzi's level of excitement. One day, we were walking along at an exceptionally brisk rate. In a move that was as sudden as it was dramatic, Suzi swerved unexpectedly and snatched up a dead bird that had been lying on the side of our path. I managed to react only after she had already picked the bird up in her mouth. By the time I could pry her jaws apart and wrestle the nastiness out of Suzi's mouth, she had already started to chew on it a little. Disgusted, I tried mightily to scrape out the remaining feathers and gristle before she could swallow them. We finished our hike and returned home.

By noon, the same day we knew Suzi was sick, no doubt, I opined, from having had the bacteria-laden bird in her mouth for a brief moment. She had the worst case of vomiting and diarrhea ever and spent all the time between episodes panting for air. The real tip-off was that she would eat nothing! That made us realize that she was seriously ill. Later that day Tanya researched the situation and came up with a veterinarian who agreed to come by the next day. Morning arrived and just before I was to leave for the office, the vet showed up. I tarried a few moments to see if he would come up with a quick diagnosis of Suzi's condition and a suggestion on how to cure it. He indicated that she had some kind of food poisoning (which we had already figured out) and said that a well-administered enema would fix her up just fine (something we had not counted on due to the tremendous bout of diarrhea she was already suffering from).

I went off to the office, relieved and glad that I did not have to witness the vet's procedure. I was accustomed to coming home for lunch and saw no reason this day to change my routine. When I arrived, I let myself into the apartment. It was very quiet, so I assumed that Suzi was by now resting in her accustomed place—the kennel and that Tanya was occupied with something in another room. I walked to the bathroom to wash up before lunch and opened the door. I could not believe my eyes! There were the veterinarian and Tanya in their underwear, Suzi and a tangle of tubes and hoses connected between Suzi and the showerhead. Everyone was in the bathtub, and everything was covered in excrement! Tanya, the vet, Suzi, and the bathtub with surrounding walls—all covered with Suzi's diarrhea! Tanya and the vet were both in the bathtub with Suzi, apparently trying to control the enema, which turned out to be wildly successful—at least in terms of harvest size. The quantity was truly awesome. I felt that no comment could possibly be appropriate, so simply closed the door and exited to another room.

Return Trip to Moscow

When it came time to move from Almaty to Moscow to take on a new long-term position there, we worried over how best to handle Suzi's trip. We didn't want her to arrive the same time as we since we planned to stay in Tanya's mother's tiny apartment temporarily while we looked for something a little more permanent. Not only was the apartment very small, we would also have many suitcases and boxes of clothing and other belongings with us. So we could visualize virtually no space at all. Plus, we didn't need the hassle with Suzi's exercise every day. I would be very busy getting acquainted with a new and extremely large project, and Tanya would have her hands full scouting for new accommodations. Thus, we made arrangements with our housekeeper in Almaty to walk with Suzi and feed her for a week while we left her in the empty apartment. Then we negotiated directly with a pilot who regularly flew the route of Almaty—Moscow. For a sum of $200 he agreed to bring Suzi to Moscow, and he promised not to put her in the luggage hold. We were afraid she would freeze to death there. So he was to pick her up from our housekeeper the morning of the flight, take her to the airport, and smuggle her into the cockpit with him. We didn't know how he planned to accomplish that and didn't feel we needed to know.

On the day she was to land in Moscow, we went to the airport as if we were marking the arrival of some important guest. We waited in the lounge; then, after a time, they announced Suzi's flight. We joined the throngs of other people meeting friends and family. In another half-hour, there appeared the pilot with whom we had made arrangements for Suzi's transit. At first, we didn't see her at all. Then we could make out that the pilot was carrying a large dark leather bag, and there was Suzi. All of her body except her head was inserted into the bag with the zipper closed right up to the back of her neck. She was looking about like a tourist and as soon as she spied us, her eyes became fixed only on us. She certainly appeared very comfortable—as if she had been traveling in a bag all her life. Very blasé! The pilot explained that he simply put her in the bag as if she were his personal luggage and set her on the floor of the cockpit. Then he opened the bag just wide enough to let her head protrude. He reported that she was very well behaved, just looked around, and kind of observed what the crew was doing. He fed her a few cookies about halfway through the flight. We welcomed our traveler and took her home, and a few days later moved into a modern, spacious apartment.

OPERATION AND AFTERMATH

Suzi was ordinarily very lively and spirited, full of energy. But about a year after we moved to Moscow, she became totally listless and apathetic. Unheard-of, she also lost her appetite. She didn't even seem anxious to go out for walks. Instead of getting excited and jumping and prancing about when I prepared her leash—the sure sign that a walk was imminent—she just stared at the floor, immobile. And when we got outside, rather than exerting herself and taking off with a stride that forced me to practically jog at the same time reining her in, she plodded along as if it were a chore. Since she had always taken such great joy from her daily walks, we realized that something was seriously wrong with her. But the loss of her appetite was the real tip-off. She had always had a voracious passion and craving for food and looked forward to her eating sessions more than anything else that occurred during her daytime routine.

Tanya asked around a bit and was recommended to contact a veterinarian who supposedly had an excellent reputation. We invited Dmitri—since that was the vet's name—to our apartment to examine Suzi and give a diagnosis. Our worries proved to be well founded. Suzi was diagnosed as being extremely ill; in fact, would die if not operated on in the very near future. She needed the equivalent of a hysterectomy. We immediately agreed to have the operation performed. Dmitri advised that he would do it in our apartment that the kitchen would serve well as his operating theater and the table itself as the specific location for the surgery. This notion left both Tanya and me feeling rather queasy to say the least. It was hard to imagine as serious an operation as this one was described to us being performed in conditions somewhat less sterile than a real operating room. It was even more difficult to visualize someone cutting Suzi open on the very table at which we took our meals.

Then there was Dmitri himself. He was tall and lanky with a swarthy face made darker by a two-day growth of whiskers. He had a long hooked nose and small, black beady eyes that fairly glimmered. He was somewhat disheveled, wore stained trousers, and a shirt that couldn't seem to stay tucked in. His shoes looked like miner's boots, and he smoked incessantly, cigarette after cigarette. But his hands appeared steady, and he didn't smell like a distillery. The most important point—he came very well recommended, and he was not only available, but he also agreed to perform the operation the very next day. Since Suzi was clearly in great distress, we agreed to have Dmitri do the surgery.

The next day Suzi lay around the apartment without any will to either eat or exercise. Tanya and I were both on edge. Dmitri was supposed to appear about 5:00 in the afternoon. When 5:30 came around with no sign of the vet, we began to get very concerned. When it got to be six o'clock our fear and anxiety levels grew exponentially. However, we reminded ourselves constantly that in Russia time means something quite different than it does back home in the States. Plus, Moscow at rush hour (actually, at all hours) was a difficult place to get around quickly. Sure enough, Dmitri showed up around 6:30. He was all business, doffing his sweater, rolling up shirtsleeves, putting his bag on the floor, and laying out instruments. Then he placed squarely in the middle of the kitchen table an elongated tin box that was very, very black. Our wonderment over what the purpose of this object was would be dissipated in short order. Dmitri opened the container which looked like a toolbox and a number of steel instruments appeared before our eyes. He picked up the implements and laid them in the tin pan. He then retrieved a bottle of vodka from his bag, unscrewed the top, took a healthy swig, and poured a large dose into the pan on top of the instruments. He then struck a match, and before we could even remark on this extraordinary activity tossed it into the pan. With a roar, the alcohol caught fire and blazed almost to the ceiling. He shrugged and mumbled, "Have to sterilize the knives." He then lit up a cigarette and asked that we bring Suzi in.

After this startling display, I tried to put on a show of confidence for Tanya's behalf and went out to carry Suzi into the kitchen. I set her on the table, which Tanya had by now covered with clean towels and exited to another room to busy myself at something that might take my mind off what was about to transpire in the kitchen. I didn't have a shred of the confidence I was pretending to exhibit in front of Tanya, but knew that I wanted no part in the play Dmitri was preparing to act out with Suzi's willing or not so willing participation. I tried to reassure Tanya that everything would be all right, but despite my best efforts, she fidgeted and fretted the entire evening. After a couple hours of this, accompanied by an eerie silence from the direction of the kitchen, I decided to retire and get some sleep if possible. Tanya stayed up to be there until Dmitri completed his task. In any event, someone had to pay his fee.

I arose early the next morning after an almost sleepless night, worried sick over Suzi, but not possessing the fortitude to actually observe what was going on. I stumbled out of the bedroom and into the hallway. There she lay, beside the threshold to her own room, stomach swathed in bandages. She was breathing shallowly and her eyes were glazed over like a fish that has been out of the water three days. There were tubes running from areas under the bandages suspended from the antlers of a moose head that hung prominently over the door to her room. I was shocked when I saw her; if it were not for the slight rise and fall of her rib cage that I could just barely make out, I would have sworn that she had already expired. Saddened, I bent over her, whispered her name, and gently stroked one flank. She actually looked at me briefly and weakly licked her lips.

Suzi lay like that for two full days. On the third, she wobbled slowly to her feet and staggered to her bowl. But she evidently didn't feel up to eating yet. She had licked a little water from a pan we brought her from time to time and now she did take a few swallows of water on her own. We actually began to feel that maybe she had a chance to survive after all. In another couple of days, she was going outside on her own and starting to snack a little on soup that Tanya specially brewed for her. In a week, she was frisky and lively, her travails almost forgotten. As for traces of the operation, she was left with a jagged scar starting from just halfway between her front legs down to just below her tail. It was big and it was ugly, but Suzi seemed to bounce back completely. A few more days and she was again ravenously hungry all the time, went out jogging, on the look-out for dogs, cats, or any other animal worth getting in a frenzy over.

Suzi's Last Days

Suzi was fine for a while, frisky and alert, always ready for a brisk walk, eternally hungry. In a few months, however, she began to show signs of listlessness. Her appetite faltered—a sure signal that something was seriously wrong. She seemed to lose her passion for the long and sometimes frenzied daily walks. Instead of spending all her time with Tanya and me when we were at home and constantly pestering us for attention, she frequently lay down in the hallway and just watched as we made our normal rounds of the apartment. For a dog that always displayed a frenetic mode of behavior, she now seemed to be lost in lethargy. She even began to show disdain for going out and total indifference toward food—despite Tanya making some of the most appetizing stews imaginable to tempt her. In a few short weeks, she had deteriorated to such a point that she could hardly get to her feet. It got to the point that I would have to physically lift her up, carry her to the lift take her downstairs and out to a nearby field, and set her down so that she could do her business. As I've said elsewhere, Suzi was not a particularly large dog, but she did make up a certain solid mass and was now a dead weight in my arms. Taking her out several times a day got to be a very laborious duty. She never ran anymore; in fact, could not even manage to walk. When she stood, she wobbled unsteadily and quivered with tremors. In a few more days, she stopped eating altogether.

Now we realized that Suzi was not just ill; we accepted the reality that she was dying. In the morning, she would wait in her kennel until I retrieved her, took her outside, and brought her back. Then she would lie on a rug in the hallway until moved by either of us. She was not tempted by any food and only licked up a couple drops of water if it were placed directly in front of her. All her joints failed her to the point where she could not even stand anymore. And from her feeble movements it was becoming evident that she was now experiencing considerable pain. As much as we agonized over the idea and hated the thought, we came to the inevitable conclusion that we had to put her to sleep.

Tanya did her natural thing of researching who could best perform the euthanasia, but totally without her natural enthusiasm. She came up with a veterinarian who, we were assured, would be considerably more professional than Dmitri. On the appointed day, the vet was supposed to appear about 5:00 p.m. Tanya's sister and brother-in-law were on hand in case we needed consoling. When asked what her plans were for the fatal moment Tanya said unequivocally that she would not be witness to the sad event. My feeling was the same. Upon reflection, however, I felt that Suzi had given us so much pleasure over the many years that it would only be fair to conduct her personally to her final resting place. So I decided that I should be on hand.

We decided that "putting her to rest" should occur in her own bedroom. Tanya had laid out a small rug on the floor there, not far from Suzi's favorite lair—her kennel. When the vet arrived, Suzi was lying on a carpet in the hallway, the only place she got to these days. Tanya's brother-in-law, the veterinarian, and I went into Suzi's room to make ready. A moment later Suzi herself appeared wobbling through the doorway. Tanya told me later that—incredible as it seemed—when we had gathered in her room, she seemed to gather strength, got to her feet, and staggered to her own bedroom as if she knew what was required and was an accepting participant in what was about to occur.

This was truly a sad moment for me, for I had sincerely and deeply cared for that animal. She had loved us without reservation, without qualification. Suzi had given the maximum of her animal devotion without ever requiring anything in return, the purest kind of dedication. Suzi approached me and collapsed onto the carpet. I cradled her head in my hands. The vet asked when he should administer the fatal injection, and I indicated right away. Suzi did not react at all to the injection itself; for by now she felt no pain whatsoever even the pinprick of that inoculation. After a few moments, however, she began visibly to weaken even more. She raised her head weakly and looked me squarely in the eyes. I tried to reassure her and gently stroked her face, purring all the time, "It's OK, Suzi." It seemed to me that her expression contained as much love and tenderness and—yes—humanity as anyone could muster. She required nothing in return; her gift was untarnished by any quid pro quo. I could see her let go; she lay back and, with a last gentle sigh, stopped breathing. I gently placed her head on the carpet, rose and left the room to tell Tanya that it was all over. A sad, sad day for us.

I have spent an undue portion of this memoir on our dog for the simple reason that she was so important a part of our stay in Almaty and later in Moscow. Without it, there would be no reminiscing about her original trip to Kazakhstan and her subsequent flight back from Almaty to Moscow. There would be no mention of her walks in the crisp Almaty mornings, her distaste of the twice-per-week baths, her bout with stomach sickness, and diarrhea. There would be no word of her operations and final succumbing to her many ailments. And most important, there would be no fond recollection of her camaraderie, her amusing antics, her unreserved loyalty, and devotion. Suzi was a faithful and dedicated companion, constant and caring—a genuine member of our family, and without her presence here this story would not be complete.

TRIP TO MOSCOW

I believe it is only fitting that I end my narrative with a "travel" story since so many of the adventures I had while living and working in the Soviet Union involved trips from one place to another. After serving for two years in Moscow on a very large US AID-sponsored project, I was invited to participate as managing director of a high-level program in Kiev. It turned out to be every bit as interesting and enjoyable as my stay in Almaty and Moscow and comprised as many fascinating anecdotes. However, this would be a subject for another chronicle as lengthy as this one, and can await its turn. The last trip I shall describe came about as a result of Tanya's and my sojourn in Ukraine and our wish to revisit her relatives in Moscow one weekend.

Getting Visas

So Tanya and I decided to go to Moscow. We hadn't been in some time, wanted to visit with friends and relatives, and I had to meet a few people on business matters. The clincher was Tanya's birthday, which was fast approaching. We figured that it would be more enjoyable to celebrate with friends and family in Moscow than by ourselves in Kiev. So we planned to combine all these elements during one long weekend. Of course, it was necessary to deal with the bureaucracy in order to receive visas. To get multiple-entry visas we would be forced to endure AIDS tests, a rather lengthy procedure, so we decided to apply for the single-entry versions, which would be simpler. Tanya performed reconnaissance at the Russian Consulate to find out what formalities had to be surmounted and when. Shortly thereafter, she returned to submit the actual applications which we had assiduously filled out in the meantime. She went back a third time to ask if they were ready. She was told that the visas were ready, but that they wouldn't be issued yet because Tanya had originally been advised that they would be ready on October 15, and had been unambiguously instructed to return on that specific date. Tanya speculated that she could pick up the visas ahead of time by simply showing up at the consulate and attempt this uncomplicated transaction on the thirteenth. As per typical Soviet bureaucracy, however, she was compelled to return again on the fifteenth to actually receive the visas. Some things never change.

We planned to take the train up on Thursday evening. This would get us into Moscow fairly early on Friday and give me, I believed, enough time for all my meetings and still allow me to be free for the entire weekend starting Friday evening. Tanya fixed a nice picnic lunch, and we boarded at the main train station in Kiev about 6:30 p.m. We departed on time and began rocking our way northward.

Lately, there had been a lot of train robberies; consequently, we had frequently been warned to keep our door locked at all times. Culprits had various creative ways of gaining entry to passengers' compartments: getting the travelers to open voluntarily by demanding to see official documents or offering to sell something at a preposterously low price or simply jimmying doors open. In one case, at least the burglars opened the door by shooting a round of AK47 bullets through it. We tried to heed the advice and kept our doors locked for most of the trip.

The Train Ride

We specially purchased tickets for the two-person coupe in order to preserve a modicum of privacy. Soon after departing Kiev, Tanya spread out the goodies she had prepared, and we made ourselves comfortable in our little cubbyhole. Russian meatballs, black bread and butter, fresh vegetables cut up into slices, and cheese and a bottle of red wine disappeared rather quickly. We read for a while and lay down on our respective berths and dozed off. About 1:00 in the morning, we were awakened by the Ukrainian border guards who banged on the door of our cabin, shone their light in our eyes, and checked out our credentials, then left. We were at the border about half an hour before we started jerkily on our way again. This tends to keep you awake. About two hours later, when we were groggily beginning to dose off, we were stopped again—this time for the Russian border guards. If you're lucky enough to doze off after the first checkpoint, it's only the super sleepers who can manage falling asleep again after the second. I'm definitely not included in that enviable class. Wouldn't you think they could be on either side of the same border and do their bureaucratic thing consecutively? No, the border check-points are about eighty miles apart.

We arrived in Moscow about 7:30 next morning—about a twelve-hour trip (Moscow being one hour ahead of Kiev). We were met by Tanya's sister—Galya, nephew—Andriusha, Galya's brother-in-law—Zhenya, and his son—Maxim who had brought two cars with them. They whisked us off to Tanya's mother's apartment where I could shave, shower, and change before going to a round of meetings for the day. Then Andriusha drove Tanya and Galya to the latter's home, and I went to Nina's (an old friend of ours, especially Tanya's, going back to her early days at Tractoroexport). I had made arrangements to see four or five people on business in Moscow that day and had requested the use of a room at Nina's store and office complex to meet with them. Trying to make five different meetings in different parts of Moscow in one working day is just about impossible. The distance and traffic will just kill you. So I tried to get the five mountains to come to Mohammed by scheduling the appointments throughout the day—but at a single venue: Nina's office.

Tanya and I have known Zhenya and his wife since early on in our relationship with one another. Maxim and Andriusha were born less than a year apart, thus grew up friends and playmates. At the time that I describe being in Moscow, they were about the same age—mid-twenties. Both were over six feet tall, weighed over two hundred and fifty pounds, were dressed in black leather jackets, both heads shaved almost to the skin. Basically, they both looked like thugs. Which, of course, they deliberately cultivated and which was definitely the fashion in the heady days of Russia's early skirmish with democracy.

Maxim had been out of work for some time, and so Galya decided that he and Zhenya could use some pick-up work. So she agreed to hire Maxim to drive me around Moscow for the day, Friday (the following week he was scheduled to take the policeman's course—which would make him a genuine thug, not just a pretend one). The only problem was that Maxim had lost his license due to some infraction, which would have normally kept him from joining the police force as well, but was overlooked on this occasion after payment of an appropriate tithe. Therefore, Zhenya came to the rescue and offered to do the driving. Maxim accompanied us since, after all, it was his "job." We left Tanya's mother's place around 9:00—plenty of time to get me to Nina's before 11:00—the time of my first meeting.

To Nina's Offices

I finally met someone I never thought I would meet in this world—someone who drives worse than Tanya. Zhenya sits up close to the front dashboard, knees nearly touching the steering wheel, and hands clutching it like it was his last connection to this earthly vale. He clenches his jaw, grits his teeth, squints his eyes, and breathes so hard he practically hyperventilates. A fur hat is firmly planted on his head, and he gives off sprays of perspiration as if he were facing the devil himself. We departed for Nina's, with the radio on at full blast playing some very unpleasant music, heat on maximum, and windows hermetically sealed. We drove along the Moscow River to the Kiev Train Station, turned right and crossed the bridge. So far, so good—except for the extreme discomforts of temperature and smell, not to mention Zhenya's hunched-over-the-wheel pose that created a state of unspeakable nervousness and foreboding in me.

When we had made it to the other side of the river Zhenya turned right so that we were now traveling parallel to the river on the opposite side, also in the opposite direction from which we had originally come. Then we took a right and another immediate right, which meant we were again traveling in the same direction as originally. Inexplicably Zhenya then turned right twice more in quick succession. This brought us back to where we had been on the bridge twenty minutes before, but needing to take a left. However, no left turns were allowed at this intersection. So we took another right which, of course, brought us back across the bridge to the train station. At this point I suggested that I would not be averse to the idea of looking for a taxi. Zhenya refused; he claimed that we would be at Nina's in twenty minutes—guaranteed!

Somehow, he made a wrong turn (could I have expected anything else at that stage?) and ended up going the wrong way along the river again. By now Maxim, who was crowded in the back began to get nervous. So he took out one of those filthy Russian cigarettes and lit up. His next statement was to ask for the map. Now I knew we were in serious trouble. Maxim's biggest contribution was to have been finding the shortest route to Nina's in record time: after all, he should have known the way in his sleep; he had worked there for four years!

It was now getting very hot in the small car. We were once again heading in the opposite direction required and were fast approaching Tanya's mother's home—our original starting point. Zhenya steadfastly refused my plea to find a taxi. He was determined to get me to Nina's himself. By now, he was sweating profusely. I should probably say at this point that Zhenya, and I never liked each other very much. At one point, I confess to having the rather uncharitable thought that Zhenya was doing everything deliberately. The thought also crossed my mind that I had somehow found myself in hell. Like Sisyphus eternally hoisting his boulder up the mountain, I was condemned to ride in a cramped car around and around the very same streets of Moscow, never arriving at my destination, endlessly crossing the Moscow River, radio playing excruciating music at full blast, heat on maximum, and the foul smell of Russian cigarettes and human sweat, riding eternally with someone I don't even like.

Sometime later, after another round of maneuvers that somehow got us back to the bridge over the Moscow River near the Kiev Train Station an hour and a half after we first crossed it, Zhenya announced triumphantly that he now recognized some land marks and knew the way for sure. Why he suddenly recognized them now, but not before when we were at the very same location I will never guess. In any event, he was right—we got to Nina's twenty minutes later. A total of two hours to travel from an apartment located twenty-five minutes away. Of course, I was late for all my appointments. But everyone is always late in Moscow so it did not matter so much. When I got out of the car I paid Maxim the agreed upon twenty dollars and politely refused his offer to drive me anywhere else when I finished my meetings later in the day.

RETURN TO KIEV

I completed my appointments for the day and met up with Tanya and her sister and other relatives. We enjoyed each others' company for the remainder of our free time in Moscow, then packed up our few belongings and prepared for the trip back to Kiev. On Sunday, Seriozha and Galya accompanied us to the Kiev Train Station for our return trip. Again a very convenient timetable, we would leave Moscow early in the evening, travel through the night, and arrive in Kiev next morning in time for me to freshen up and get to the office only a couple hours later than I was accustomed to starting work.

The Insurance Scam

Since well before we actually moved to Kiev we were aware of a little scam border guards, customs agents, and anyone else who thought he might get away with it try to work on foreigners. They approach new arrivals at border crossings and demand to be shown proof of medical insurance. When the foreigner is not able to produce any (since most people naturally do not think of carrying such a document around with them), they cite Ukrainian law and insist that the hapless traveler immediately buy temporary insurance from them. They usually charge around three dollars per day that the new arrival intends to stay—normally one to three weeks—which is not too lofty a sum for the victim and quite a nice haul for the perpetrator. Most foreigners do not resist unduly. Many are first time visitors and will accept pretty much anything that is not truly outrageous. Others have no idea of Ukrainian law and so acquiesce. Still others shrug it off and chalk it up the cost of doing business there. Up to now, Tanya and I had managed to come into and out of Ukraine several times without even being approached.

On our way back to Kiev from Moscow, we were awakened at the first (Russian) checkpoint—everything was as expected: a cursory inspection of our documents, a twenty-minute wait while the border guards visited every other passenger on the train and a jerky start up toward the next destination. At the Ukrainian side over an hour later, when we were groggily handing over our documents to be checked, a civilian joined the border guards. He demanded that we show proof of insurance. I always let Tanya handle situations like these. She politely advised the man that we did, of course, have insurance, but that, unfortunately, we did not have any proof of that with us. He abruptly discontinued the conversation, took our passports and other documents and disappeared. This was calculated to intimidate and soften us up. He returned in five minutes with another man—a big, burly guy in a black leather coat who was obviously the enforcer. The two of them tried to persuade us that we had no choice other than to purchase insurance. They kindly offered to sell it to us directly thus saving us the inconvenience of leaving the train, going into the terminal, and acquiring it at a kiosk there.

I believe Tanya and I would probably have resisted the scam on principle alone. However, these two ruffians started to become more and more obnoxious. We demonstrated numerous documents that proved that we were on government contract, that we are required to have insurance, but that we are not required to carry proof of same. The conversation began to get heated. The two guys left, all our documents with them. Our normal fifteen-to-twenty minute stop at the border had already become half an hour with the clock still ticking. They came back a third time, now with a tall, thin man with mustache and long leather coat—the uniform of choice for gangsters here. This guy was obviously the head intimidator. By now, it had become a matter of principle with them. They again demanded an insurance payment, and we noted that they never named a specific figure. They were obviously willing to negotiate. When we again refused, the sinister one said, "Well, then, we will have to take you off the train." At which point Tanya, who had by now lost her patience and diplomatic manner, jeered at them, "And what will you do with us then?" This caused a lengthy pause and an equally lengthy silence. We all knew that they had to be bluffing; they had simply not encountered foreigners with as much resistance as we had showed. After another minute or so, Mr. Mustache threw our documents at us, turned around and stormed off, followed by his two companions. They hated to lose face but realized, at last, that they were simply not going to get anywhere with us. They saw us if not as seasoned travelers then at least not as neophytes. Soon thereafter, the train jolted forward, and we were on our way once again. We did not sleep the rest of the way to Kiev—but we did laugh a lot.

A METAPHOR FOR RUSSIA

In a sense, this experience was a metaphor for my considerable time spent in the Soviet Union and later Russia as well as other former republics. People we encountered exhibited a multitude of flaws, but they were very human ones that caused as many laughs as laments. The entire system they existed in was defective; it forced citizens to circumvent the strict application of the law and discover other, frequently grey-area, means of survival. Russians were possessed of a very human, humorous, and witty side in an otherwise grim existence. The governing bureaucracy appeared monolithic and unshakable but was extremely vulnerable. Russians could find a way out of practically any seemingly insurmountable situation. The ingrained bureaucracy created endless boredom; great swaths of time were wasted on totally useless endeavors. But given half a chance, Russians exhibited a boundless creativity that could be used to circumvent regulations as easily as to produce incredible works of art or heroism—whichever the case might be. My life there was endlessly fascinating, full of the unexpected, equally causing heartache as well as exhilaration. It is a country and a people that are both memorable and impressive. A beautiful, humane people oppressed by over seventy years of the excruciatingly stifling influence of Soviet bureaucracy.

And when given the slightest chance the humanity would peek out from behind the bureaucratic facade and manifest itself in ways sometimes benevolent, sometimes humorous, sometimes kindhearted, and always endearing.

www.ingramcontent.com/pod-product-compliance
Lightning Source LLC
Chambersburg PA
CBHW061337280526
45784CB00001B/44